Basic Vocabulary™

Clothing

Al Bullock
Barbara Cleghorn
Margery Fraser
Paul Frewen
Pat Mills
Audrey Soutar

Skill Areas:	Vocabulary
Ages:	5 thru 11
Grades:	K thru 5

LinguiSystems, Inc.
3100 4th Avenue
East Moline, IL 61244-9700
1-800 PRO IDEA
1-800-776-4332

FAX: 1-800-577-4555
E-mail: service@linguisystems.com
Web: www.linguisystems.com
TDD: 1-800-933-8331
(for those with hearing
impairments)

Printed in the U.S.A.

ISBN 0-7606-0489-4

About the Authors

Front row: Paul Frewen, Barbara Cleghorn, Pat Mills
Back row: Margery Fraser, Al Bullock, Audrey Soutar

At the time of the writing of the *Basic Vocabulary* series, the authors were a group of six classroom teachers at inner-city schools in Ottawa, Ontario. Their teaching experiences range from kindergarten to eighth grade in a wide variety of schools and classroom situations. They have been involved in delivering regular graded programs to classes with extremely high percentages of English as a Second Language students. It is in this area that the authors are particularly qualified to assist other classroom teachers who require support for students at the beginning and middle levels of language acquisition.

Illustrations by Ken Prestley – Blue Sky Communications
Page Layout by Silver Oaks Communications
Cover Design by Lisa Parker

Table of Contents

Introduction

Basic Vocabulary – Clothing has been developed by classroom teachers for classroom teachers. It is intended to help students develop sight word vocabulary as they work independently or as part of a group. It can be used by students for vocabulary development, as well as for English as a Second Language instruction.

This book concentrates on one theme — Clothing. The vocabulary within the book progresses from simple to difficult, and words introduced in one unit might appear in later units to build your students' understanding of those words. Level 1 is for students ages 5 – 8. Level 2 is for students ages 8 – 11. Level 2 is divided into two parts. Part 1 is a review of the vocabulary introduced in Level 1. Part 2 introduces your students to new vocabulary related to the theme.

This practical, ready-to-use series requires little preparation and can be used alongside other programs. *Basic Vocabulary – Clothing* allows you to:

- provide your students with an immediately useful, sight-based vocabulary with a thematic approach

- provide a modified program to meet students' individual needs

- build language acquisition with individuals, small groups, and entire classrooms

The variety of activities and approaches used to address an array of learning styles and the simple directions allow you to send activity sheets home to involve parents. Students use writing, cutting and gluing, and visual recall to build their vocabulary. Also, each set of directions is written to the students so they can follow along as you read. Specific types of activities include:

Pictures in Context – Each unit begins by introducing the vocabulary in the context of a picture scene.

Words in Isolation – Students identify, match, read, write, and spell the sight vocabulary.

Sentence Completion – Students use their newly acquired vocabulary within correct syntax.

Following Directions – Students demonstrate comprehension skills by following directions.

The Extension Activities provide additional worksheets related to the theme. The Vocabulary Picture Cards can be copied or mounted onto heavier paper, cut apart, and colored by your students and used as flash cards. They can also be used to play Concentration or Lotto. You might also enlarge the individual pictures and have students place the cards on the actual items in your classroom (e.g., place the *desk* card on a desk).

The key to *Basic Vocabulary – Clothing* is its comprehensive, repetitive approach to new language acquisition and its flexibility to meet your needs. You choose which activities to use with your students and in what order they are to be completed. However you choose to use the materials in this book, though, we hope that you and your students work together to build better language and basic vocabulary skills.

Al, Barbara, Margery, Paul, Pat, and Audrey

Vocabulary List

Weather

cloud	lightning	sunny
cloudy	rain	thunderstorm
cold	rainbow	warm
cool	rainy	weather
fog	snow	wet
foggy	snowy	wind
hail	sun	windy
hot		

It's Hot

cap	sun hat
sandals	swimsuit
shorts	T-shirt
socks	

Accessories

belt	necklace
bracelet	ring
earrings	tie
glasses	umbrella

School Clothes

blouse	shirt
dress	shoes
pants	skirt
raincoat	sweater

It's Cold

boots	mittens
gloves	scarf
hat	snowpants
hood	snowsuit
jacket	

Bits and Pieces

buckle	laces
button	patch
collar	pocket
cuff	zipper

Other Words Used

a	day	has	my	the
and	draw	her	orange	these
are	earmuffs	here	purple	this
around	Friday	his	red	Thursday
black	girl	I	Saturday	towel
blue	go	is	see	Tuesday
boy	goes	it	she	Wednesday
brown	graph	like	Sunday	white
can	green	likes	sunglasses	yellow
color	he	Monday	sunscreen	

Weather 1

Name _____

Print each word.

 sunny

 cloudy

 windy

 snowy

 rainy

 foggy

Weather 2

Name _____

Cut out these weather symbols to use on page 9.

Weather 2, cont.

Name _____

Keep track of the weather using the symbols from page 8.

Sunday	Monday	Tuesday	Wednesday	Thursday	Friday	Saturday

Weather 2, cont.

Graph the weather from page 9.

Weather Graph

Weather 3

Name _____

Cut out the clothes and glue them on the girl.

Dressing for Cool Weather

cap

jacket

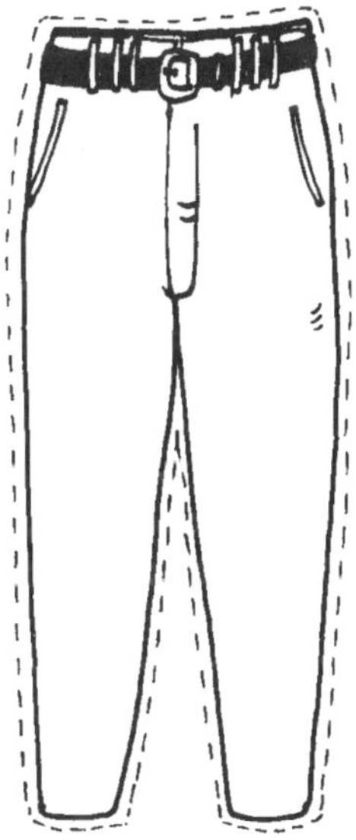

pants

shoes

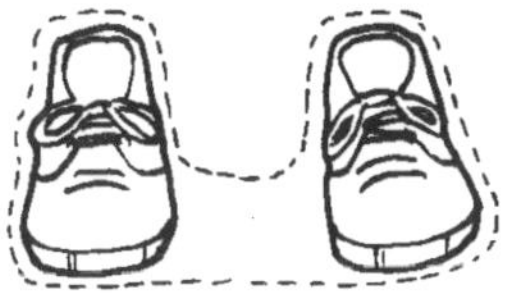

Cut out the items and glue them on the boy.

Dressing for Rainy Weather

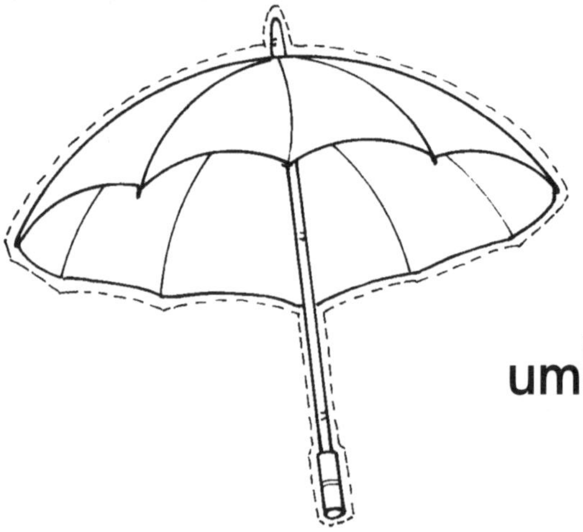

umbrella

raincoat

boots

Cut out the items and glue them on the boy.

Dressing for Hot Weather

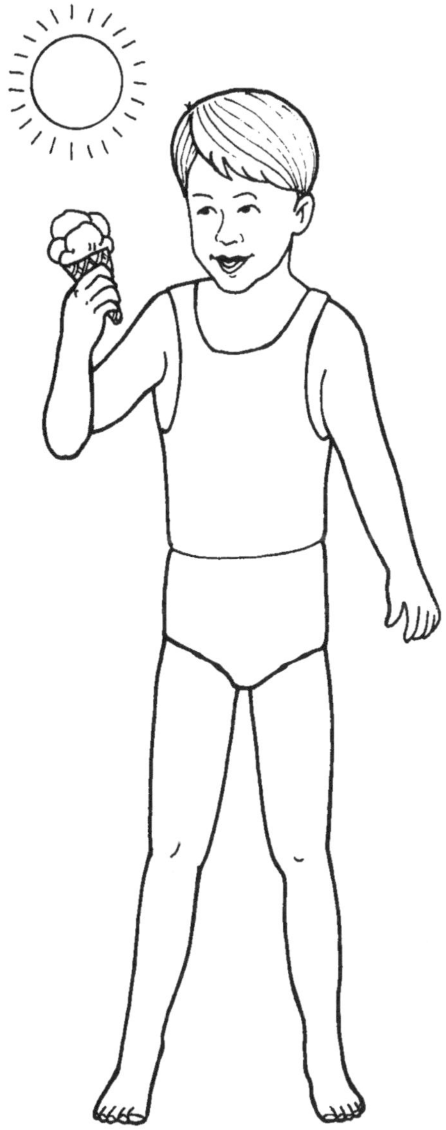

cap

T-shirt

shorts

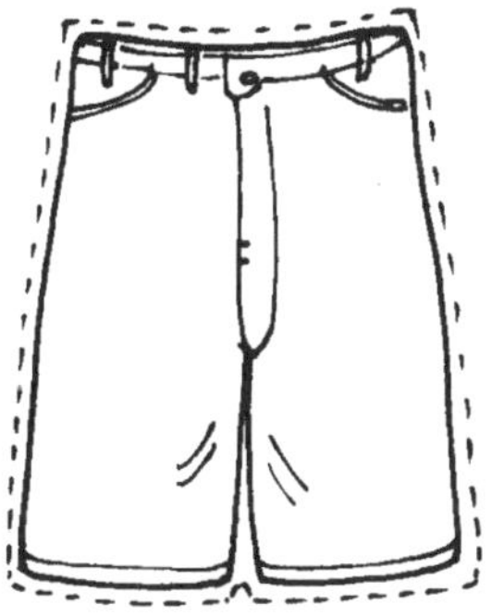

sandals

Name _____

Cut out the items and glue them on the girl.

Dressing for Cold Weather

mittens

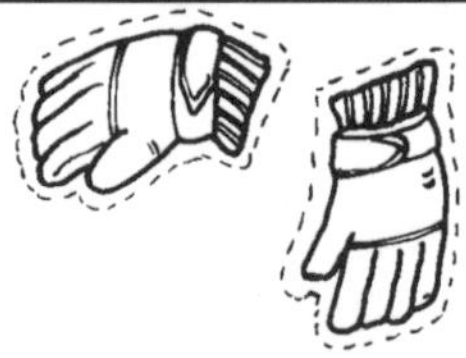

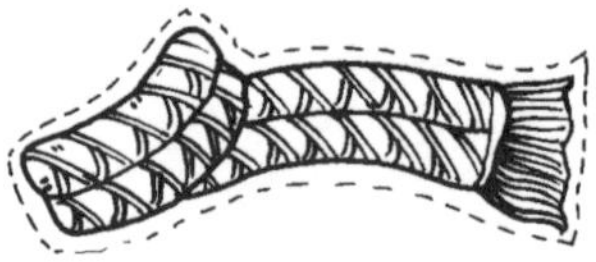

scarf

earmuffs

hat

snowsuit

boots

Cut out the items and glue them on the boy.

Dressing for the Beach

cap

sunscreen

towel

sunglasses

swimsuit

sandals

Weather 4

Name _____

Circle each thing that's wrong in this picture.

Read these thunderstorm **do's** and **don'ts**.

Don't stand under trees.
Don't stand on high places.
Don't go near fallen wires.
Don't go swimming.
Do go to shore if in a boat.
Do go inside.

Don't use the telephone.
Don't use electrical appliances.
Don't go near windows.
Don't take a bath or shower.

Weather 6

Name _____

Match the weather with the clothes.

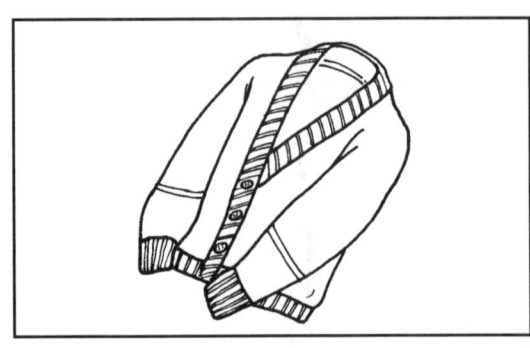

Use the weather words to complete the puzzle. Then, print each word.

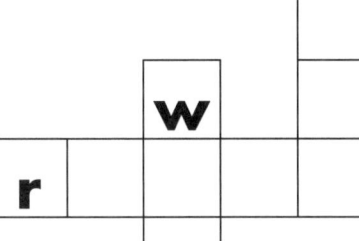

foggy _____

sunny _____

cloudy _____

windy _____

rainy _____

snowy _____

School Clothes 1

Read the word for each object pictured.

dress

shirt

sweater

raincoot

pants

blouse

shoes

skirt

School Clothes 1, cont.

Name _____

Print the word for each object pictured.

School Clothes 2

Print each word.

dress

skirt

blouse

shirt

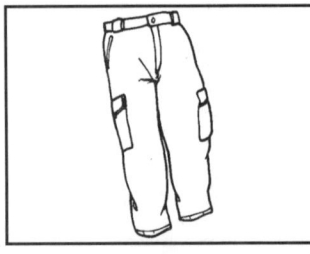

pants

shoes

School Clothes 3

Name _____

Color the pictures to match the descriptions. Then, print the correct word under each picture.

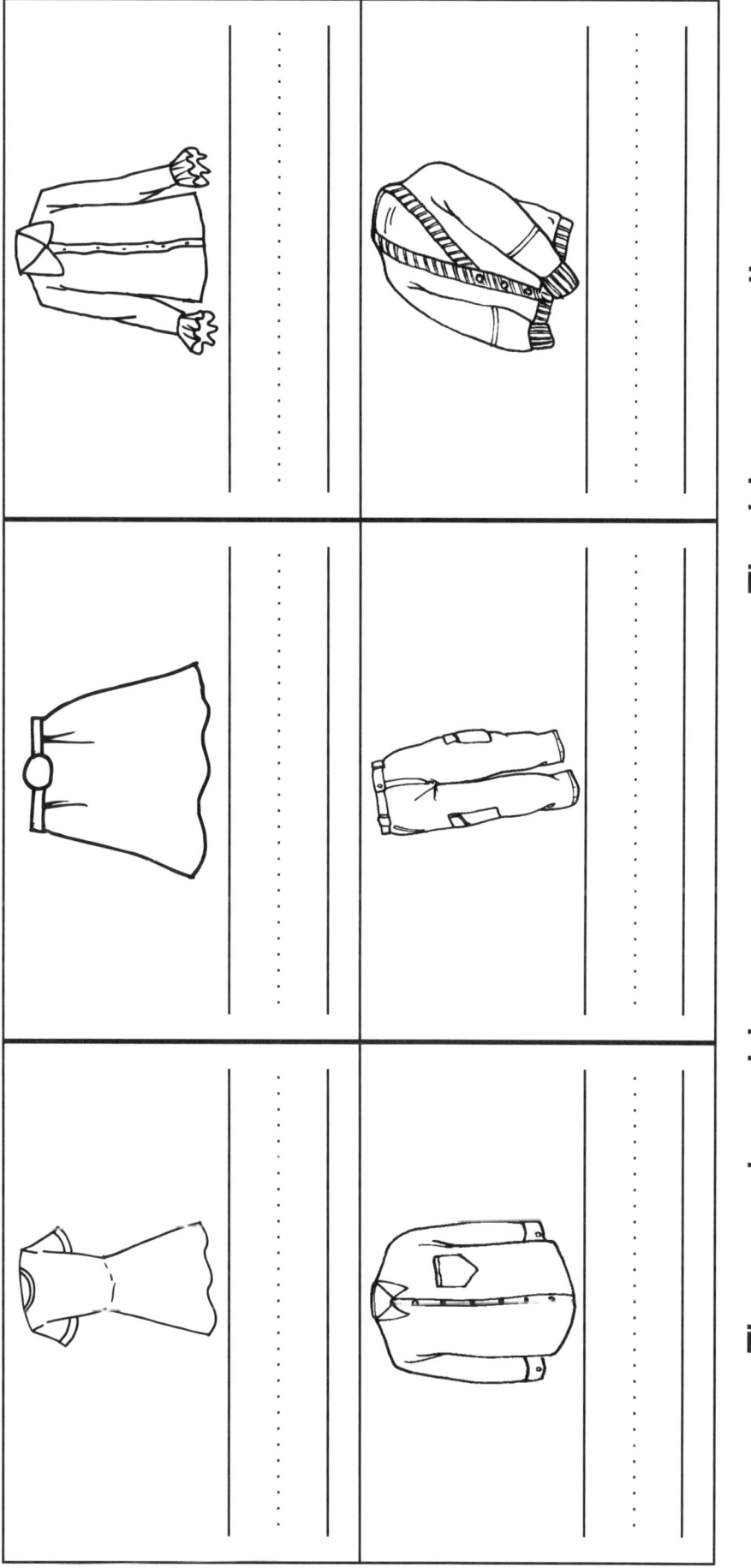

1. The sweater is blue.
2. The skirt is green.
3. The pants are brown.
4. The blouse is yellow.
5. The shirt is white.
6. The dress is orange.

Name _____

Draw a picture for each sentence.

Here is the red dress.

Here is the blue skirt.

Here are the yellow pants.

Draw a picture for each sentence.

Here are the green shoes.

Here is the orange sweater.

Here is the purple raincoat.

Name _____

Complete each sentence.

 I like my _____ .

 I like my _____ .

 I like my _____ .

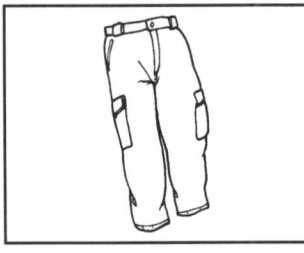 I like my _____ .

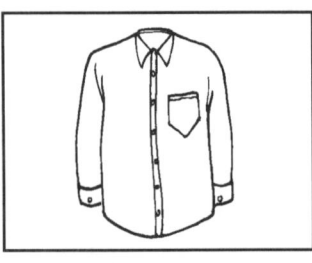 I like my _____ .

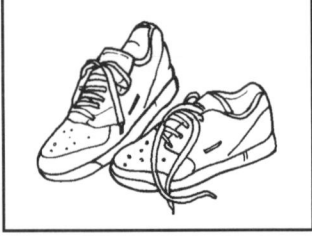 I like my _____ .

Name _____

Print the correct word under each picture.

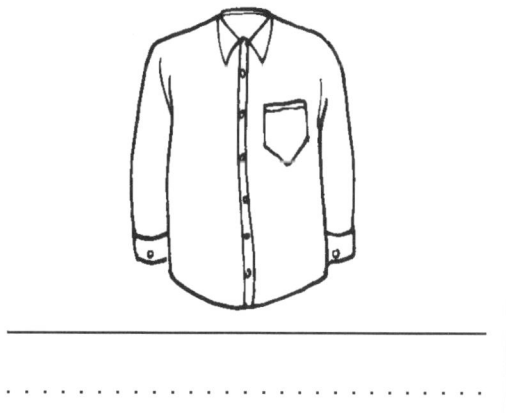

sweater

shirt

raincoat

dress

shoes

pants

It's Hot 1

Name _____

Read the word for each object pictured.

sun hat

swimsuit

cap

T-shirt

shorts

socks

sandals

It's Hot 1, cont.

Print the word for each object pictured.

Print each word.

 shorts

 T-shirt

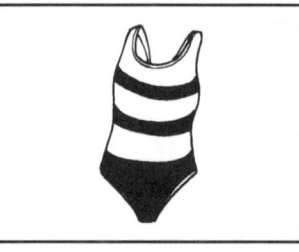 swimsuit

 sandals

 sun hat

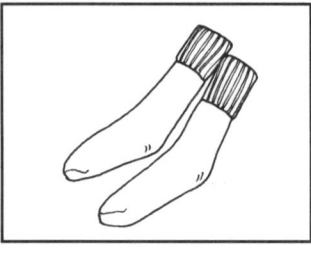 socks

Name _____

Print each word.

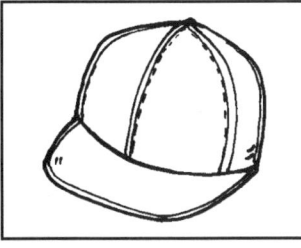

cap

dress

blouse

skirt

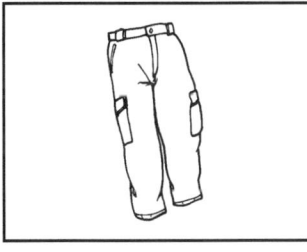

pants

shoes

Name _____

Cut out each picture and glue it by the correct word. Then, print each word.

	__shorts__ ....
	__swimsuit__ ....
	__sandals__ ....
	__socks__ ....
	__cap__ ....
	__T-shirt__ ....

Cut out each picture and glue it by the correct word. Then, print each word.

	sun hat
	dress
	blouse
	pants
	shirt
	shoes

Name _____

Cut out each picture and glue it by the correct word. Then, print each word.

	sweater
	raincoat
	dress
	pants
	shirt
	shoes

Name _____

Complete each sentence with **her** or **his**.

girl — This is <u>her</u> dress.

boy — This is <u>his</u> shirt.

his   her

1. This is _____ dress.

2. This is _____ shirt.

3. This is _____ sweater.

4. This is _____ blouse.

5. This is _____ cap.

6. This is _____ sun hat.

Draw a picture for each sentence.

This is his blue shirt.

This is his orange cap.

This is her red sun hat.

Draw a picture for each sentence.

This is her purple blouse.

This is his yellow sweater.

This is her green dress.

Print the correct word under each picture.

_____

. . . .

_____

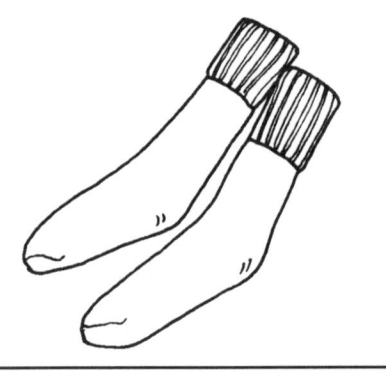

T-shirt

shorts   cap

socks   sandals

sweater

_____

. . . .

_____

_____

. . . .

_____

It's Hot 7

Name _____

Circle the words on the right that are spelled correctly.

shorts	shrots	shorts	sorhts	shorts
	hortss	shorts	shorts	storhs
sandals	sandals	slandas	sandals	
	lndsas	sandals	danslas	
socks	sckos	socks	ckoss	socks
	socks	skocs	socks	sokcs
cap	cap	pac	acp	cap
	pca	cap	cap	acp
dress	derss	dress	desrs	dress
	drses	drsse	dress	dress
pants	pnats	pants	pants	spant
	pants	napts	stanp	pants

Answer each question with **yes** or **no**.

yes   no

1. Is this a dress?

_____

2. Is this a skirt?

_____

3. Is this a blouse?

_____

4. Is this a sweater?

_____

5. Is this a shirt?

_____

Answer each question with **yes** or **no**.

yes   no

6. Is this a raincoat?

_____
·······················
_____

7. Is this a T-shirt?

_____
·······················
_____

8. Is this a swimsuit?

_____
·······················
_____

9. Is this a sun hat?

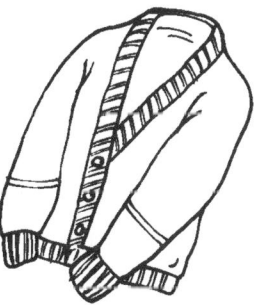

_____
·······················
_____

10. Is this a cap?

_____
·······················
_____

It's Hot 9

Use the picture clues to complete the puzzle.

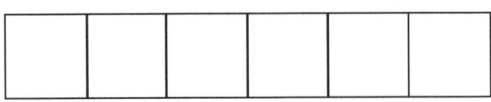

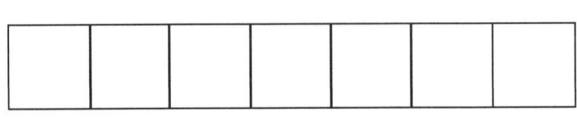

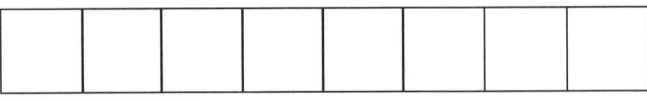

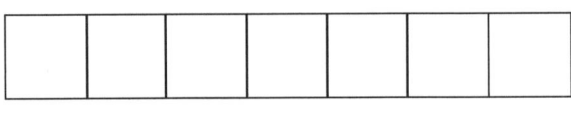

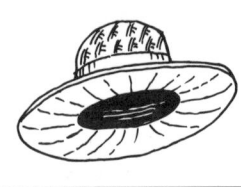
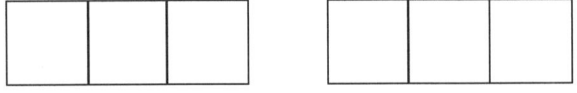

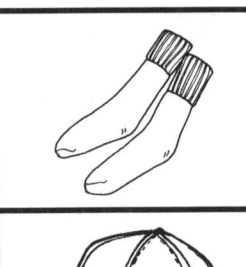
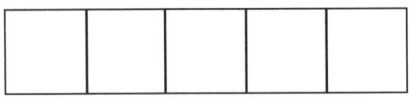

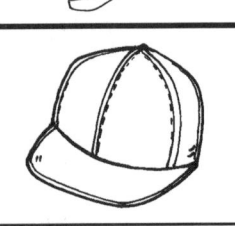
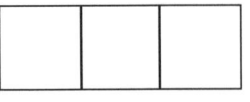

swimsuit   shorts   cap   T-shirt
sandals   socks   sun hat

Name _____

Read the word for each object pictured.

hood

scarf

snowsuit

boots

gloves

hat

mittens

jacket

snowpants

It's Cold 1, cont.

Name _____

Print the word for each object pictured.

It's Cold 2

Name _____

Print each word.

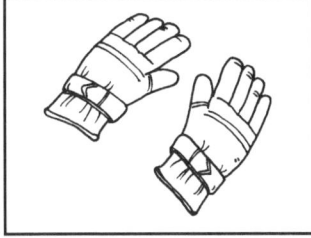 gloves

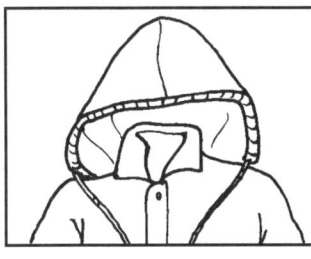 hood

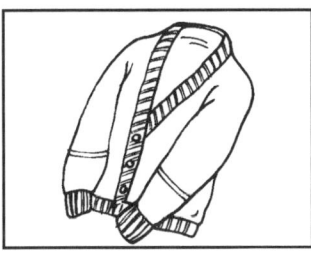 sweater

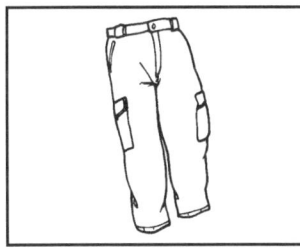 pants

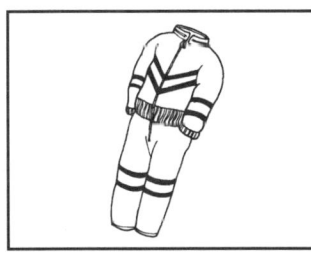 snowsuit

 skirt

Print each word.

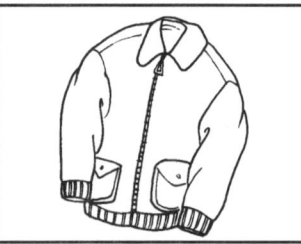 jacket

 boots

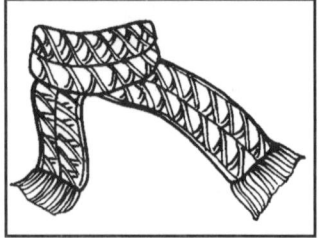 scarf

 hat

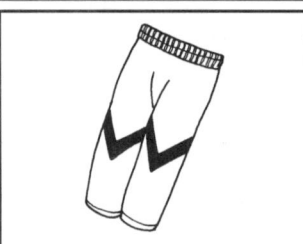 snowpants

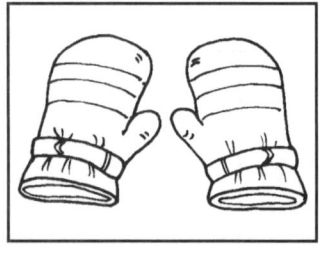 mittens

It's Cold 3

Name _____

Cut out each picture and glue it by the correct word. Then, print each word.

☐	snowsuit
☐	jacket
☐	scarf
☐	hood
☐	gloves
☐	mittens

 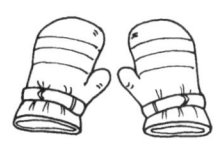   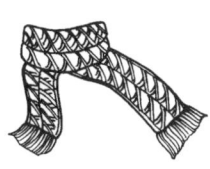 

Name _____

Cut out each picture and glue it by the correct word. Then, print each word.

<u>snowpants</u>

<u>shoes</u>

<u>raincoat</u>

<u>boots</u>

<u>dress</u>

<u>socks</u>

It's Cold 4

Name _____

Color the pictures to match the descriptions. Then, print the correct word under each picture.

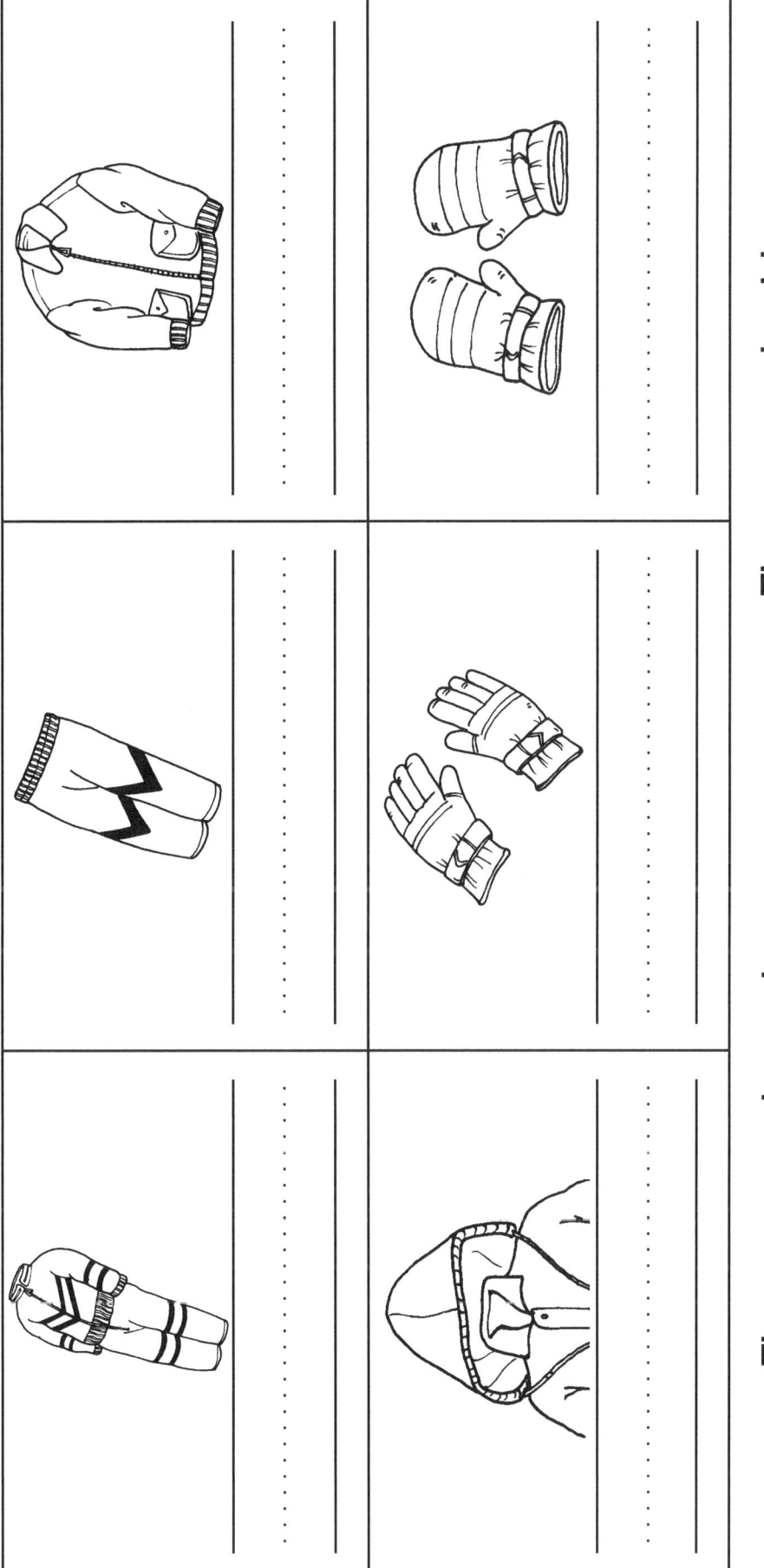

1. The snowpants are brown.
2. The mittens are red.
3. The jacket is green.
4. The snowsuit is blue.
5. The gloves are purple.
6. The hood is orange.

It's Cold 5

Name _____

Print the correct word under each picture.

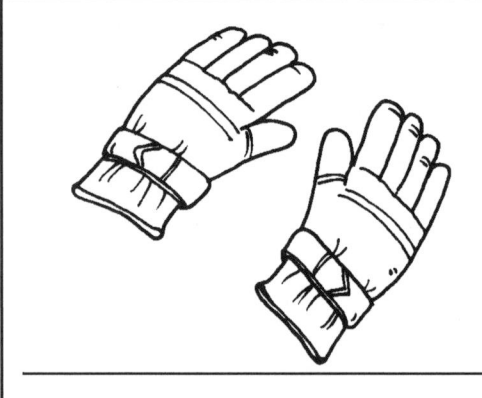

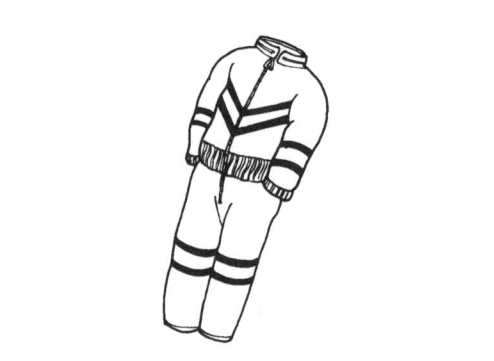

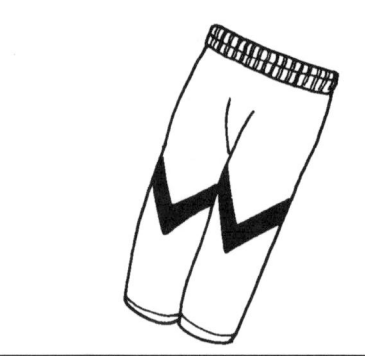

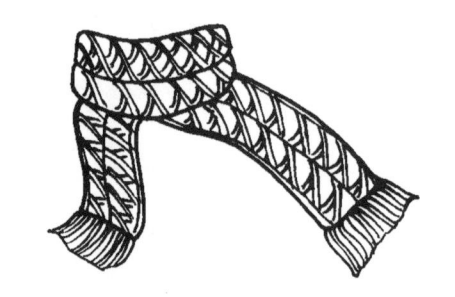

snowsuit

scarf

snowpants

boots

hat

gloves

Complete each sentence.

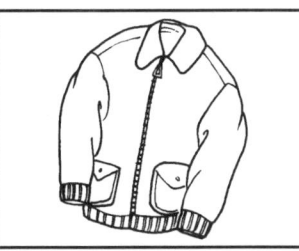 See the _____ .

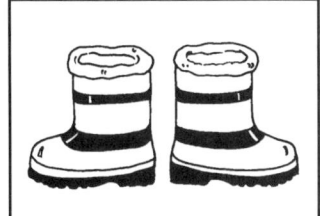 See the _____ .

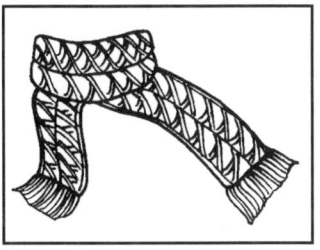 See the _____ .

 See the _____ .

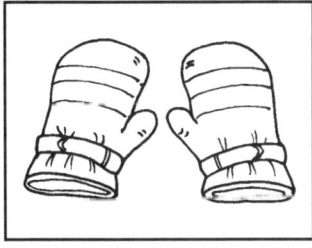 See the _____ .

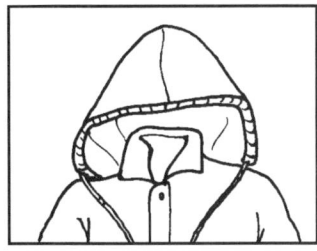 See the _____ .

Complete each sentence.

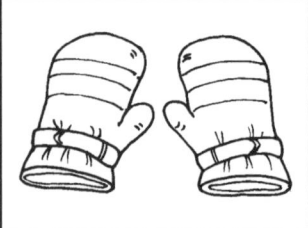 See the _____ .

(shorts   mittens)

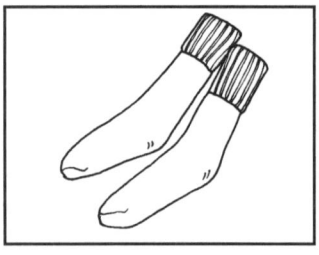 See the _____ .

(sandals   socks)

 See the _____ .

(boots   swimsuit)

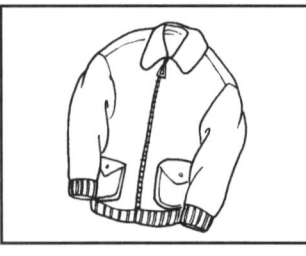 See the _____ .

(jacket   hood)

 See the _____ .

(hat   snowpants)

Complete each sentence.

See the _____.

(T-shirt   skirt)

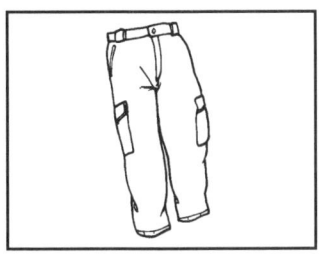

See the _____.

(raincoat   pants)

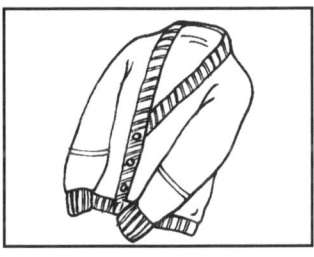

See the _____.

(skirt   sweater)

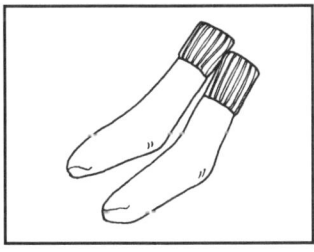

See the _____.

(socks   shoes)

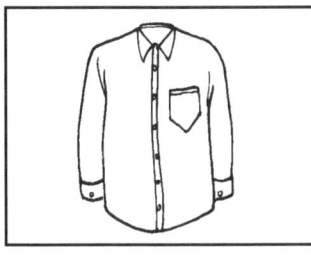

See the _____.

(dress   shirt)

It's Cold 8

Name _____

Look at the pictures and complete each sentence with **she** or **he**.

He   She

1. _____ has a jacket.

2. _____ has snowpants.

3. _____ has boots.

4. _____ has a scarf.

5. _____ has a hat.

Look at the pictures and complete each sentence with **she** or **he**.

girl · She · she | boy · He · he

He   She

1. _____ has mittens.

2. _____ has gloves.

3. _____ has a hood.

4. _____ has a snowsuit.

It's Cold 9

Draw a picture for each sentence.

She has a red jacket.

He has a blue snowsuit.

He has black boots.

Name _____

Draw a picture for each sentence.

She has a yellow scarf.

He has a purple hat.

She has green mittens.

It's Cold 10

Name _____

Print each word in the correct column.

A Hot Day	A Cold Day

swimsuit
T-shirt
gloves
snowsuit

scarf
mittens
sun hat
shorts

jacket
sandals
cap
snowpants

Name _____

Read the word for each object pictured.

necklace

earrings

glasses

bracelet

tie

belt

umbrella

ring

Accessories 1, cont.

Print the word for each object pictured.

Name _____

Print each word.

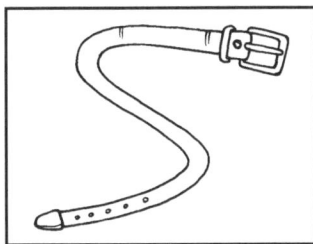 belt

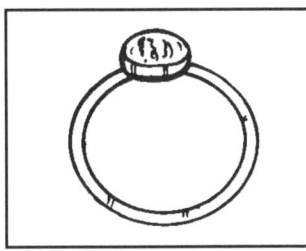 ring

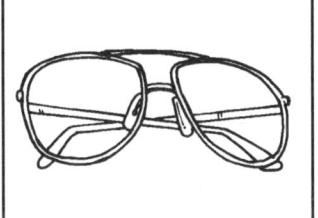 glasses

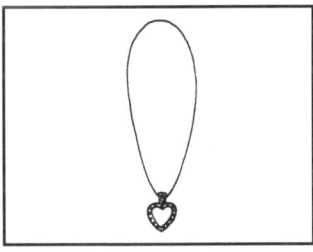 necklace

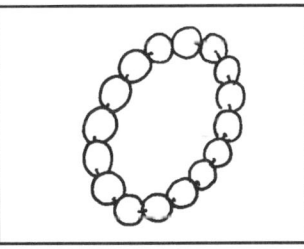 bracelet

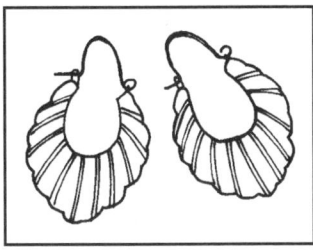 earrings

Name _____

Print each word.

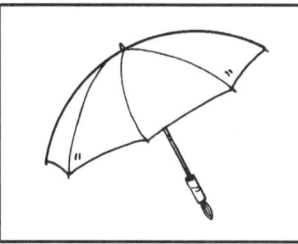 umbrella

 tie

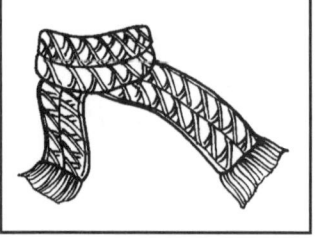 scarf

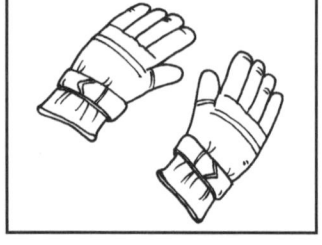 gloves

 hat

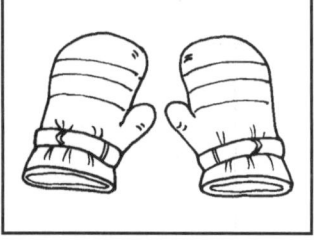 mittens

Name _____

Cut out each picture and glue it by the correct word. Then, print each word.

earrings _____

bracelet _____

sweater _____

sandals _____

blouse _____

socks _____

  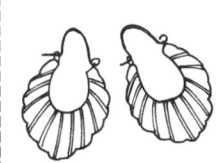   

Name _____

Cut out each picture and glue it by the correct word. Then, print each word.

	umbrella
	belt
	tie
	ring
	glasses
	necklace

     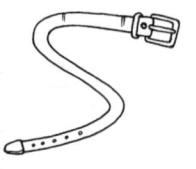

Accessories 4

Name _____

Color the pictures to match the descriptions. Then, print the correct word under each picture.

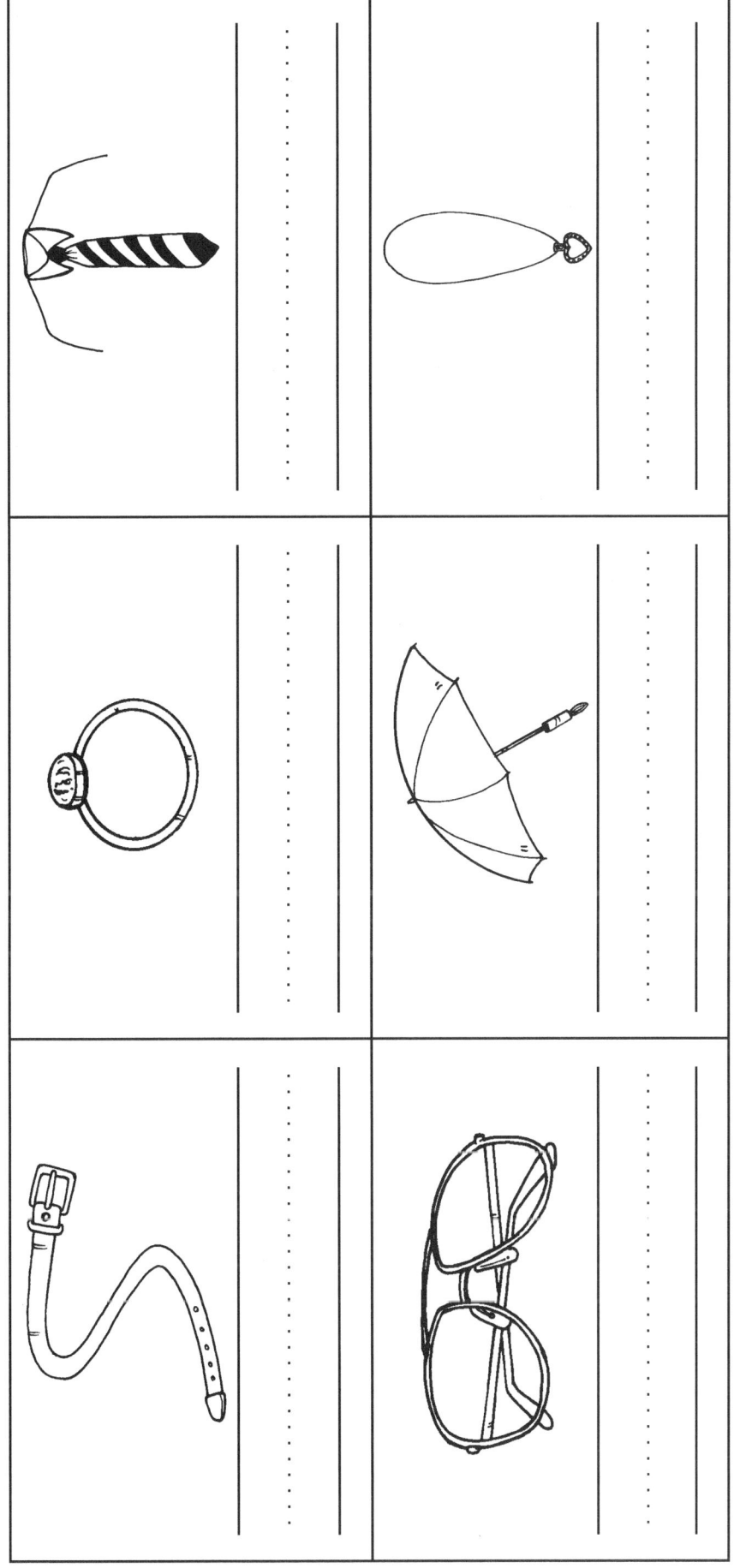

1. The umbrella is red and blue.
2. The tie is green.
3. The belt is brown.
4. The glasses are purple.
5. The necklace is orange.
6. The ring is yellow.

Name _____

Draw a picture for each sentence.

He has his ring.

She has her earrings.

He has his yellow tie.

Name _____

Draw a picture for each sentence.

He has a green belt.

She has her purple umbrella.

She has her orange glasses.

Accessories 6

Name _____

Complete each sentence.

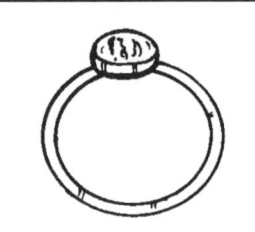 She likes her _____ .

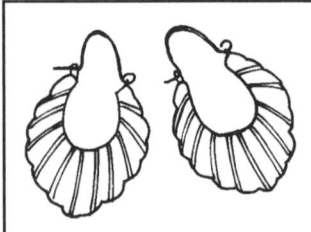 She likes her _____ .

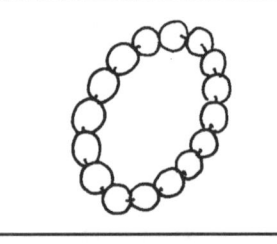 She likes her _____ .

 He likes his _____ .

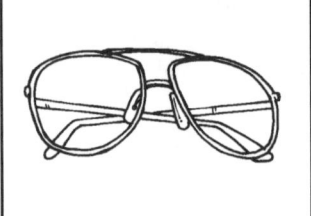 He likes his _____ .

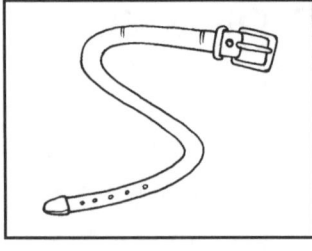 He likes his _____ .

Print each word under the correct picture.

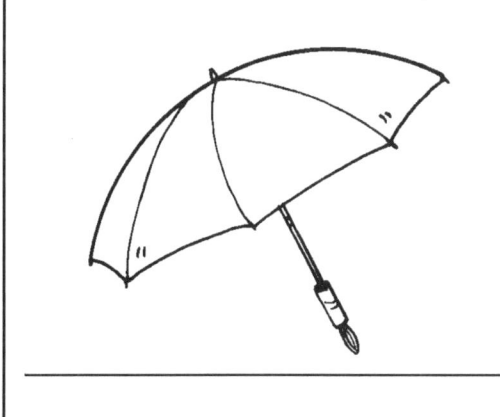

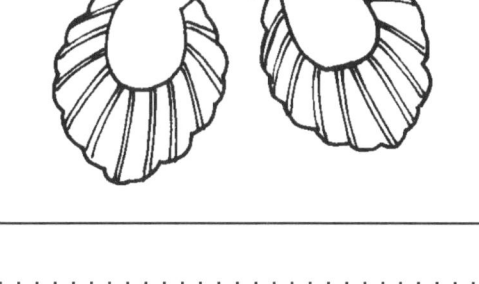

bracelet

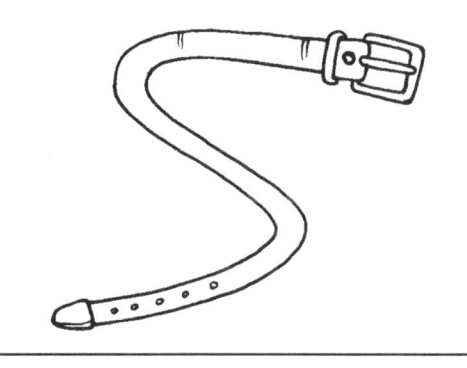

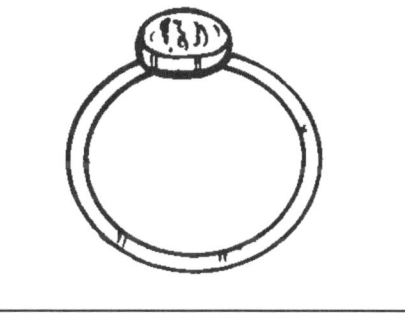

earrings

belt

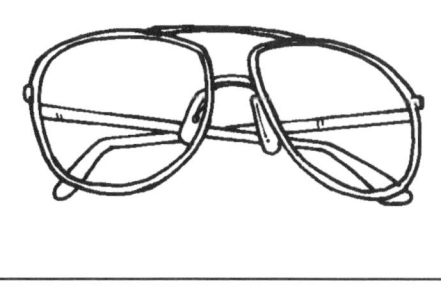

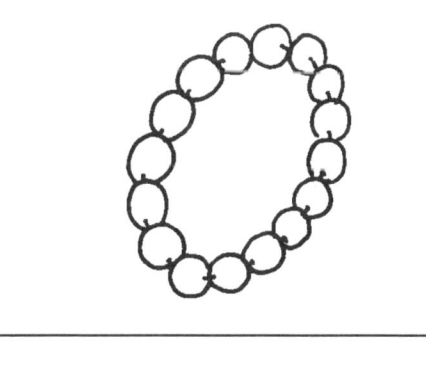

umbrella

ring

glasses

Accessories 8

Name _____

Draw a line to match each picture with the correct word. Then, print the word.

 •   • | tie | ....
 •   • | necklace | ....
 •   • | glasses | ....
 •   • | umbrella | ....
 •   • | earrings | ....
 •   • | belt | ....
 •   • | bracelet | ....
 •   • | ring | ....

Accessories 9

Name _____

Print **yes** if you agree with each statement. Print **no** if you disagree.

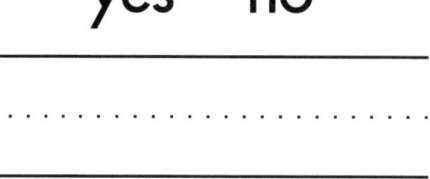

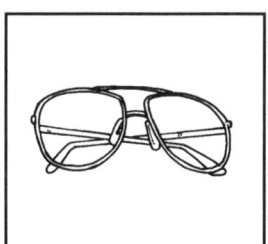 1. Here is a belt.

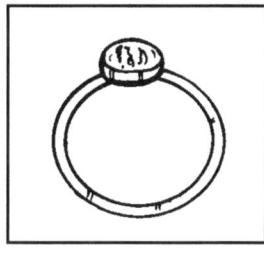 2. Here is a ring.

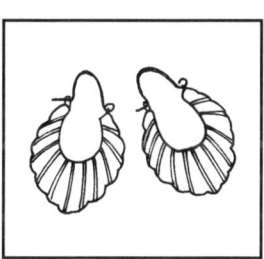 3. Here are earrings.

 4. Here is a necklace.

 5. Here is an umbrella.

Name _____

Print **yes** if you agree with each statement. Print **no** if you disagree.

yes   no

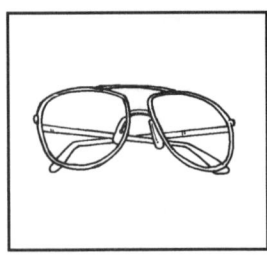

1. Here are the glasses.

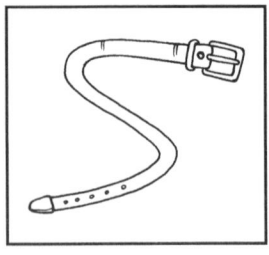

2. Here is an umbrella.

3. Here is a tie.

4. Here is a ring.

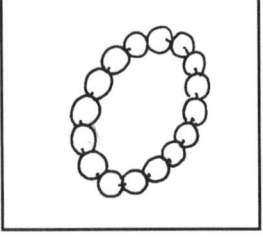

5. Here is a bracelet.

Read the word for each object pictured.

button

collar

buckle

pocket

cuff

zipper

patch

laces

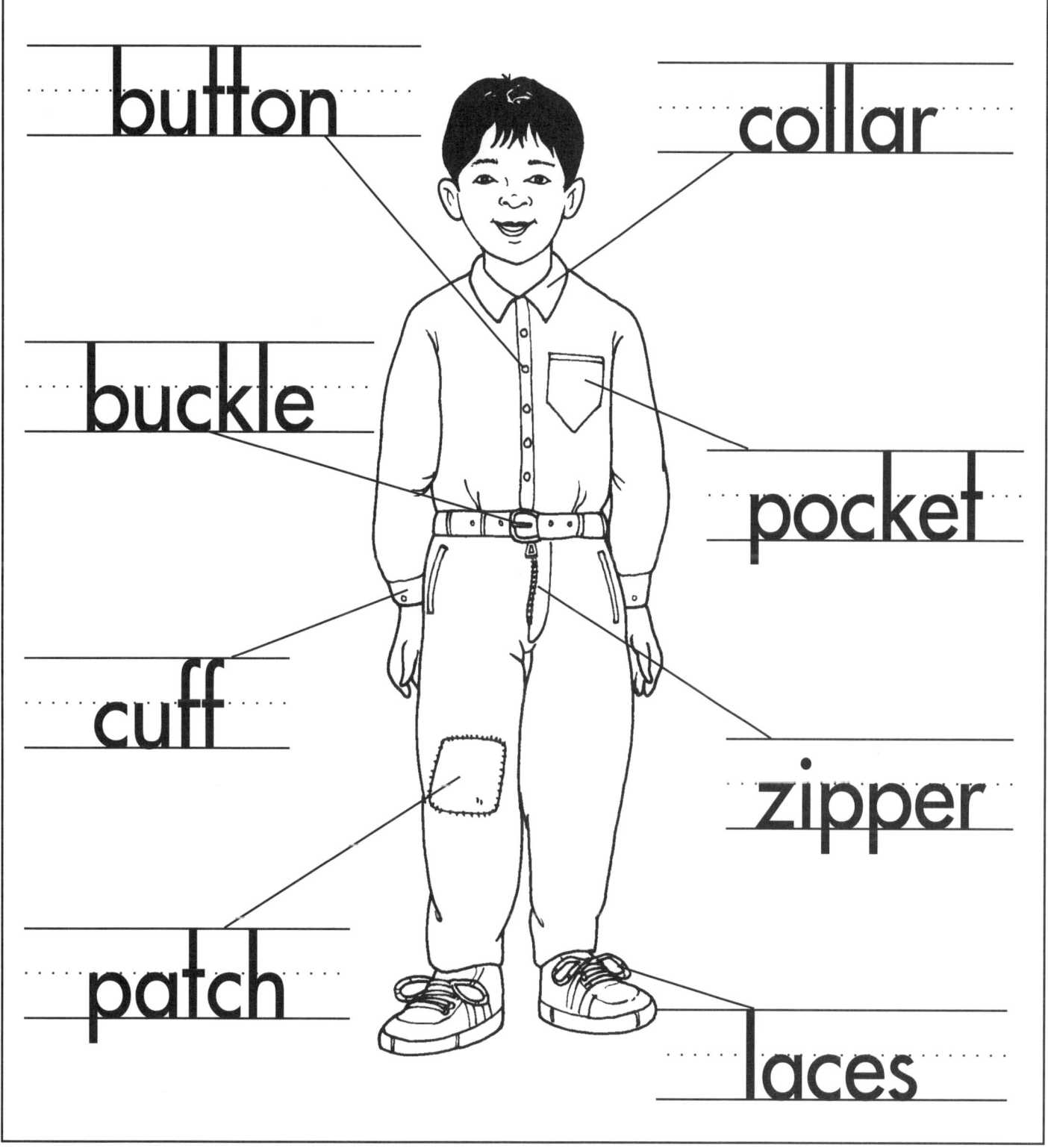

Print the word for each object pictured.

_____

· · · · · · · · · · · · · · · ·

_____

_____

· · · · · · · · · · · · · · · ·

_____

_____

· · · · · · · · · · · · · · · ·

_____

_____

· · · · · · · · · · · · · · · ·

_____

_____

· · · · · · · · · · · · · · · ·

_____

_____

· · · · · · · · · · · · · · · ·

_____

_____

· · · · · · · · · · · · · · · ·

_____

Bits and Pieces 2

Name _____

Print each word.

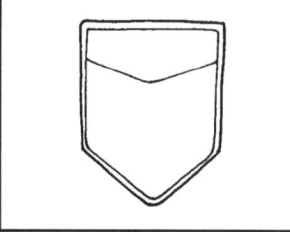
pocket

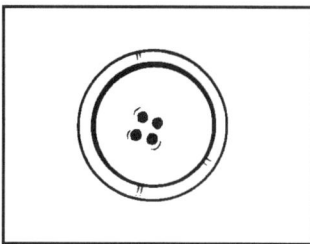
button

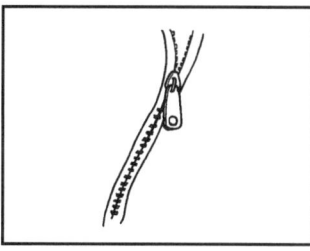
zipper

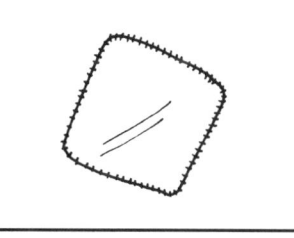
patch

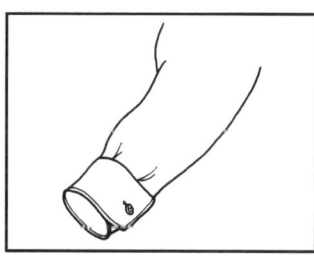
cuff

laces

Print each word.

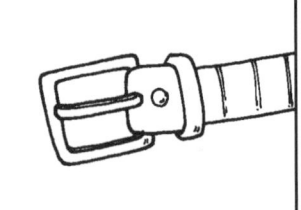 buckle

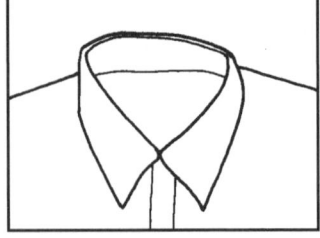 collar

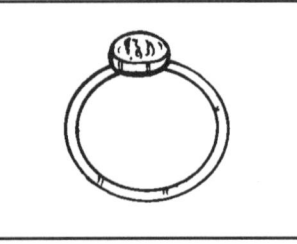 ring

 tie

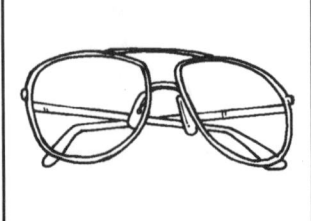 glasses

 umbrella

Name _____

Cut out each picture and glue it by the correct word. Then, print each word.

buckle ....

collar ....

button ....

pocket ....

zipper ....

laces ....

   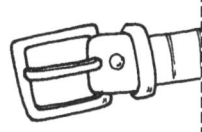 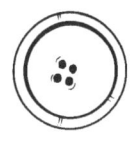 

Level 1
Basic Vocabulary – Clothing
77

Bits and Pieces 4

Print the correct word under each picture.

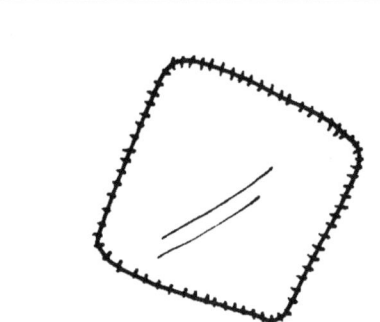

_____

. . . .

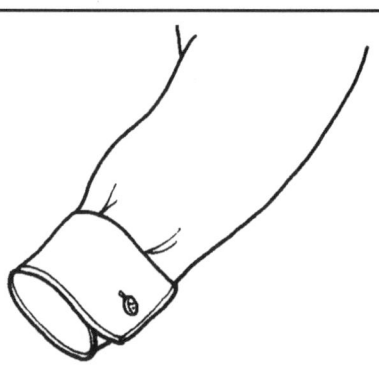

_____

. . . .

patch

cuff   laces

zipper   button

pocket

_____

. . . .

_____

. . . .

Complete each sentence.

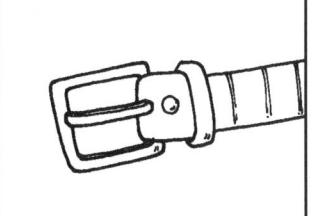 I can see a _____ .

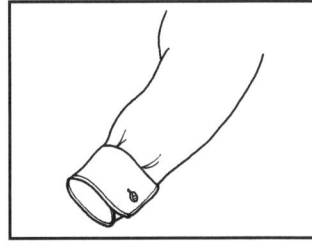 I can see a _____ .

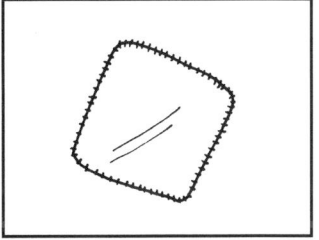 I can see a _____ .

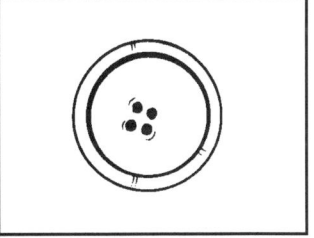 I can see a _____ .

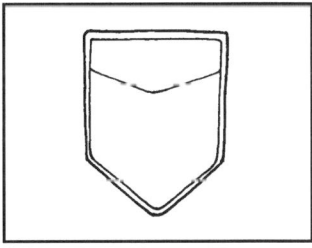 I can see a _____ .

 I can see _____ .

Bits and Pieces 6

Color the pictures to match the descriptions.   Then, print each word.

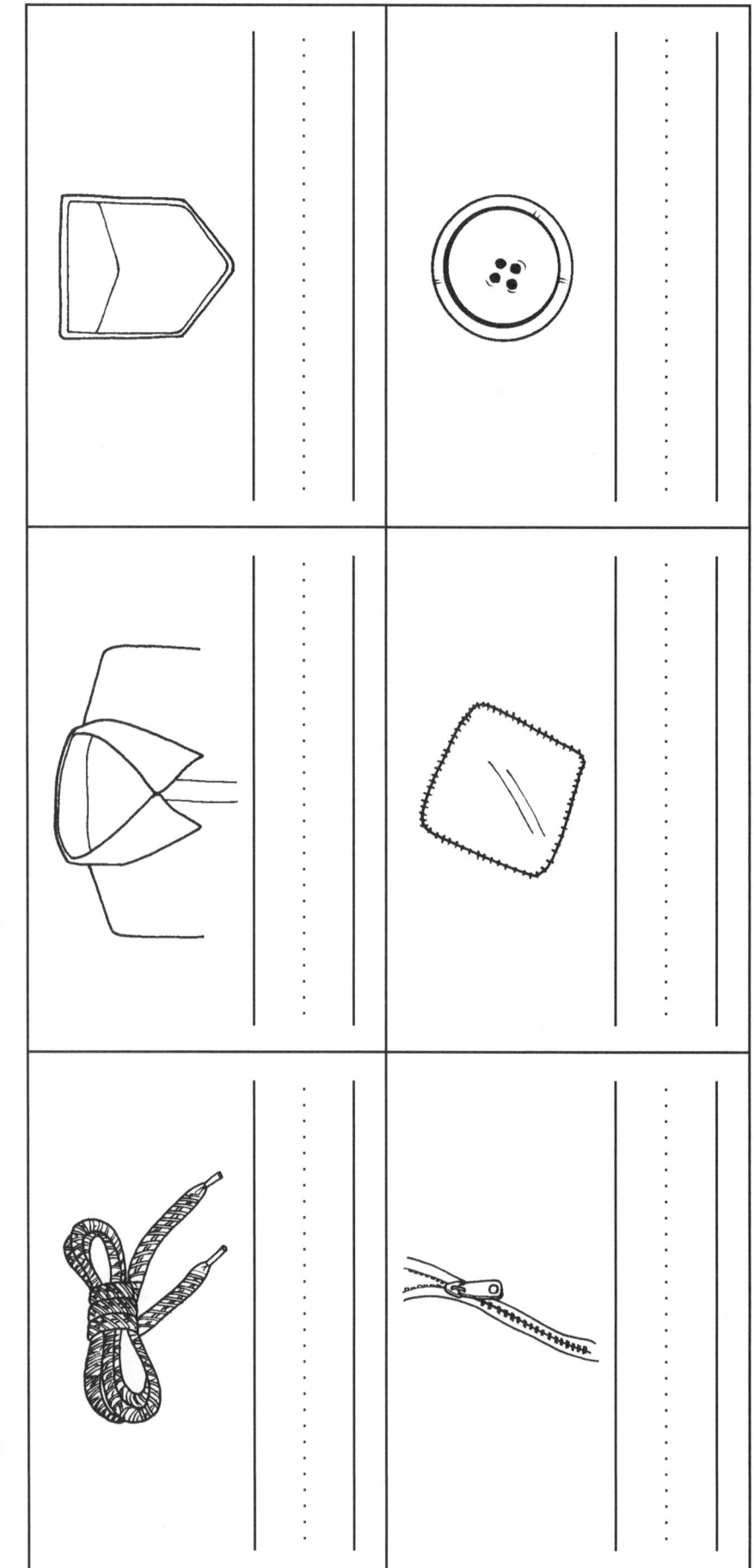

1. The pocket is blue.
2. The collar is pink.
3. The patch is green.

4. The laces are yellow.
5. The zipper is purple.
6. The button is orange.

Bits and Pieces 7

Name _____

Print each word under the correct picture.

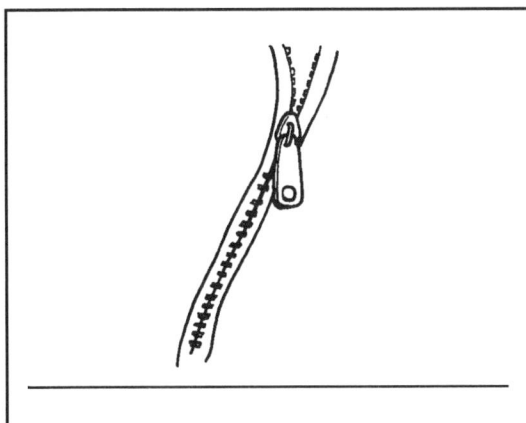

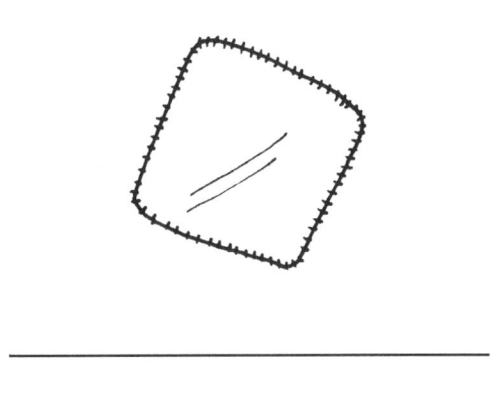

pocket

buckle

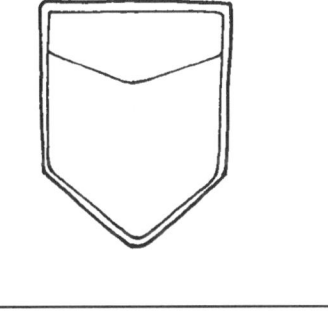

zipper

patch

collar

button

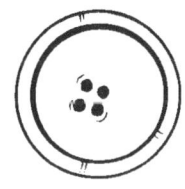

Bits and Pieces 8

Name _____

Follow the directions.

Draw a pocket. Color it blue.

Draw a button. Color it yellow.

Draw a buckle. Color it orange.

Follow the directions.

Draw a collar. Color it blue.

Draw a patch. Color it brown.

Draw a zipper. Color it red.

Name _____

Draw a picture for each sentence.

He has a green belt.

She has her purple umbrella.

She has her orange glasses.

Bits and Pieces 10

Name _____

Look at the pictures to complete each sentence.

1. I like her
   (ring   glasses)

2. I like her
   (bracelet   pocket)

3. I like his
   (necklace   glasses)

4. I like her
   (tie   earrings)

5. I like his
   (pocket   ring)

6. I like his
   (umbrella   collar)

7. I like her
   (umbrella   pocket)

8. I like his
   (bracelet   tie)

9. I like her
   (necklace   buckle)

10. I like his
    (belt   ring)

11. I like his
    (necklace   buckle)

Print **yes** if you agree with each statement. Print **no** if you disagree.

The belt is **around** her waist.

yes   no

1. A belt goes around the waist.

2. An umbrella goes around the leg.

3. A ring goes around the finger.

4. Laces go around the arm.

5. A pocket goes around a dress.

6. A necklace goes around the neck.

7. A collar goes around the neck.

8. A bracelet goes around the hips.

9. A button goes around a shirt.

10. A tie goes around the neck.

Vocabulary List

belt	hood	shoes
blouse	jacket	shorts
boots	laces	skirt
bracelet	mittens	snowpants
buckle	necklace	snowsuit
button	pants	socks
cap	patch	sun hat
collar	pocket	sweater
cuff	ring	swimsuit
dress	raincoat	tie
earrings	sandals	T-shirt
glasses	scarf	umbrella
gloves	shirt	zipper
hat		

School Clothes 1

Read the word for each object pictured.

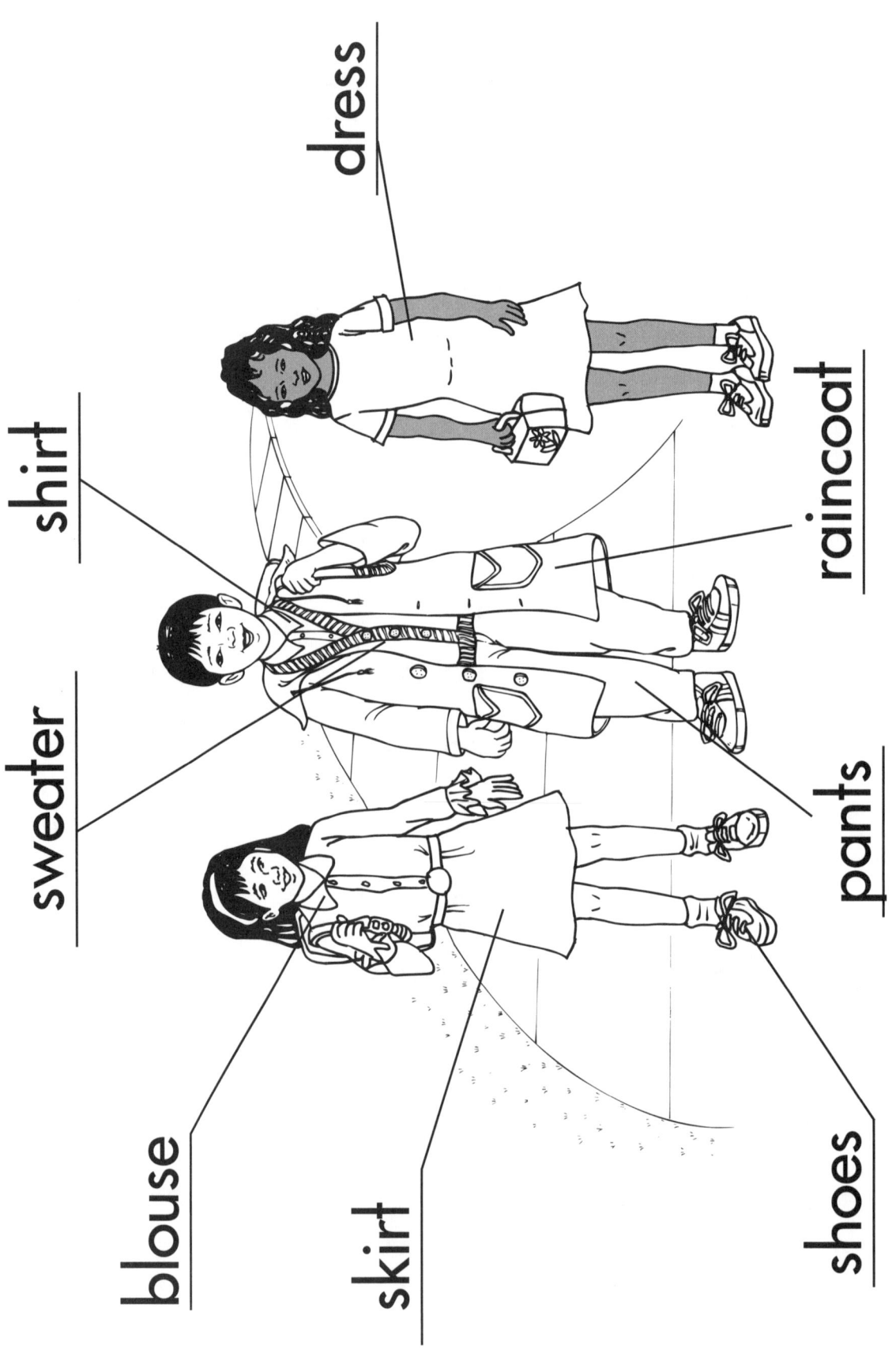

shirt

sweater

blouse

skirt

dress

raincoat

pants

shoes

School Clothes 1, cont.

Write the word for each object pictured.

School Clothes 2

Here are some words for you to use.

dress

skirt

blouse

shirt

pants

shoes

sweater

raincoat

Name:

Write the word for each object.

_____

_____

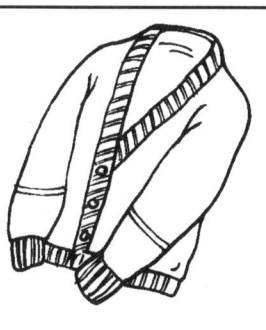

_____

_____

_____

_____

_____

_____

School Clothes 3

Color the pictures to match the descriptions. Then, write the correct word under each picture.

1. The sweater is blue.
2. The skirt is green.
3. The pants are brown.
4. The blouse is yellow.
5. The shirt is white.
6. The dress is orange.

School Clothes 4

Complete each sentence.

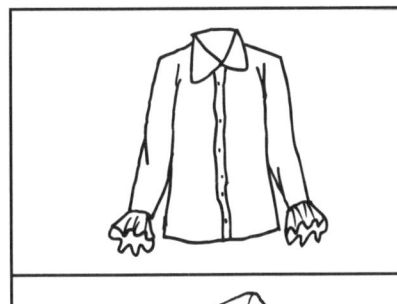

I like my _____.

I like my _____.

I like my _____.

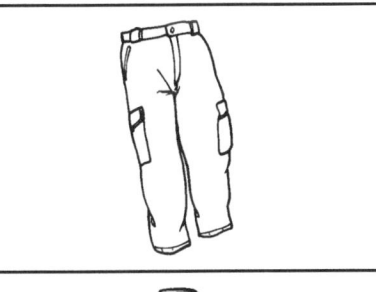

I like my _____.

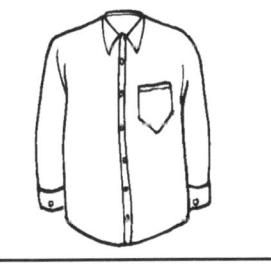

I like my _____.

I like my _____.

Name: _____

Complete each sentence with **her** or **his**.

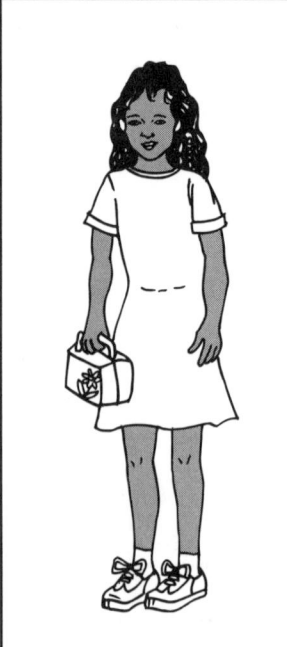

This is
<u>her</u> dress.

This is
<u>his</u> shirt.

This is _____ dress.

This is _____ shirt.

This is _____ sweater.

This is _____ blouse.

This is _____ cap.

This is _____ sun hat.

School Clothes 6

Circle the correct answer.

1. Which one of these is not worn by boys?
   a. shirt   b. dress   c. shoes
   d. sweater   e. raincoat

2. Which one of these keeps us dry in a rain storm?
   a. raincoat   b. blouse   c. sweater
   d. pants   e. shoes

3. Which one of these has two legs?
   a. dress   b. skirt   c. shoes
   d. pants   e. raincoat

4. Which one of these does not have sleeves?
   a. dress   b. raincoat   c. skirt
   d. blouse   e. sweater

5. Which one of these has laces?
   a. pants   b. sweater   c. shirt
   d. dress   e. shoes

6. Which one of these is usually knit?
   a. raincoat   b. sweater   c. blouse
   d. shirt   e. shoes

Name:

Fill in the blank.

1. Mom wears a _____ when it rains.

2. That _____ looks nice with a green blouse.

3. Dad put a _____ over his shirt to keep warm.

4. The top of her long _____ is blue.

5. He has a new _____ and tie.

6. She buttons her frilly, silk _____ at the back.

7. He bought yellow laces for his new running _____ .

8. The boys wear long _____ to school.

dress
skirt
sweater
pants
raincoat
blouse
shirt
shoes

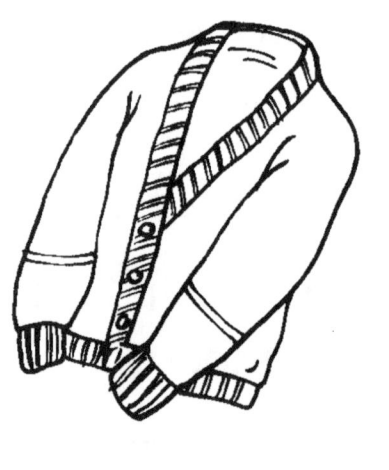

It's Hot 1

Read the word for each object pictured.

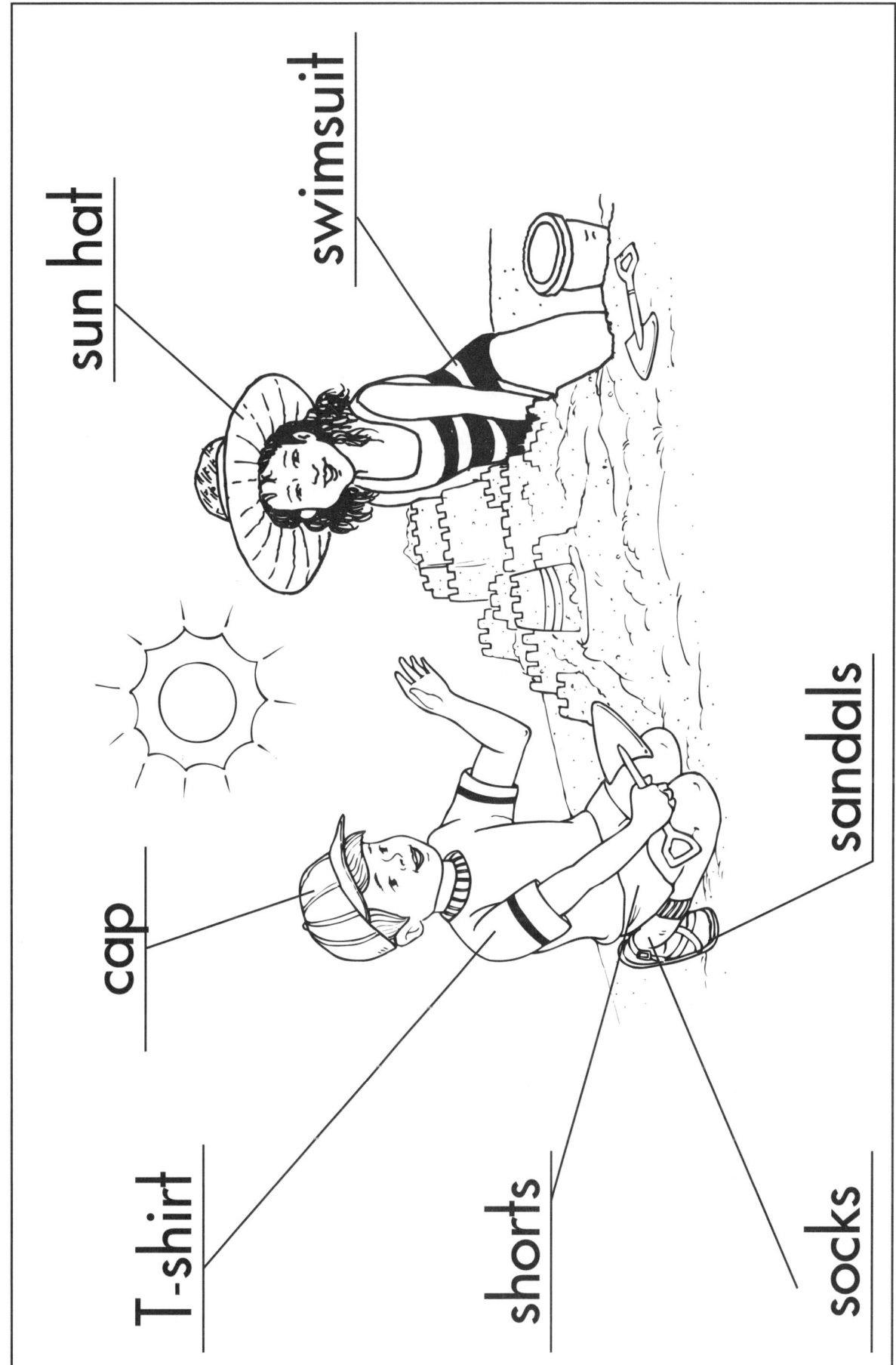

sun hat

swimsuit

cap

T-shirt

shorts

sandals

socks

It's Hot 1, cont.

Write the word for each object pictured.

It's Hot 2

Name:

Here are some words for you to use.

shorts

T-shirt

swimsuit

sandals

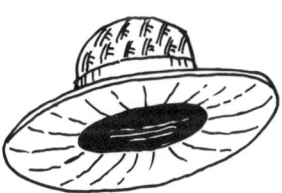

sun hat

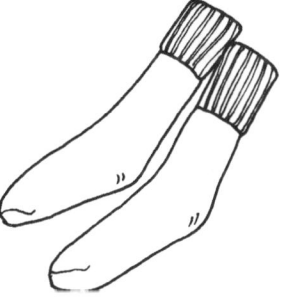

socks

cap

Name:

Write the word for each object.

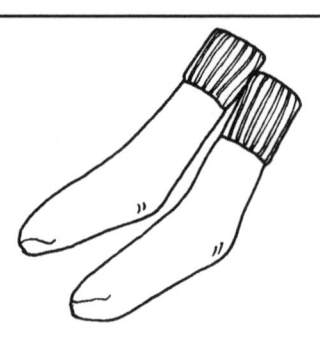

_____

_____

_____

_____

_____

_____

_____

Answer each question with **yes** or **no**.

yes   **no**

1. Is this a dress?

_____

2. Is this a skirt?

_____

3. Is this a blouse?

_____

4. Is this a sweater?

_____

5. Is this a shirt?

_____

6. Is this a raincoat?

_____

7. Is this a T-shirt?

_____

8. Is this a swimsuit?

_____

9. Is this a sun hat?

_____

10. Is this a cap?

_____

It's Hot 4

Name:

Circle the correct answer.

1. Which one of these do you wear to go swimming?
    a. socks
    b. dress
    c. swimsuit
    d. shoes
    e. raincoat

2. Which one of these do you wear on your feet?
    a. shirt
    b. blouse
    c. swimsuit
    d. shorts
    e. socks

3. Which one of these do you wear on your head?
    a. sun hat
    b. shorts
    c. sandals
    d. blouse
    e. sweater

4. Which one of these is worn by a baseball player during a game?
    a. swimsuit
    b. cap
    c. sandals
    d. shorts
    e. raincoat

5. Which one of these has two legs?
    a. shirt
    b. cap
    c. sandals
    d. shorts
    e. socks

6. Which one of these is a kind of shoe?
    a. shorts
    b. sweater
    c. sandals
    d. T-shirt
    e. sun hat

It's Hot 5

Name: _____

Fill in the blank.

1. He wears _____ and a T-shirt to the gym.

2. Mom put on her new two-piece _____
   and went swimming.

3. He takes off his socks when he wears _____
   on his feet.

4. She put a ribbon and flowers on her straw _____.

5. Dad wears a _____ on his head when he plays baseball.

6. There are holes in the toes of his white _____.

7. The sleeves of her _____ are dirty.

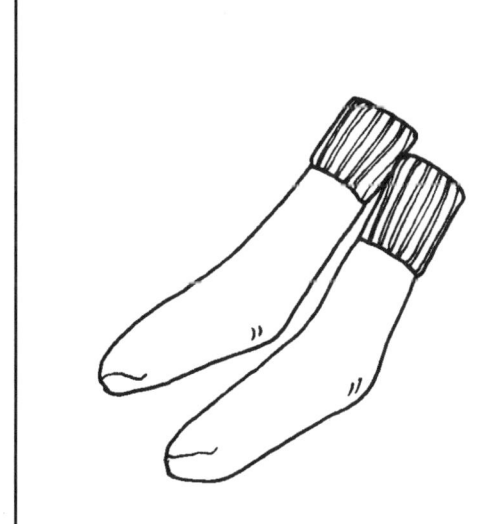

T-shirt
swimsuit
sandals
shorts
sun hat
socks
cap

It's Cold 1

Read the word for each object pictured.

hood

scarf

snowsuit

boots

gloves

jacket

hat

mittens

snowpants

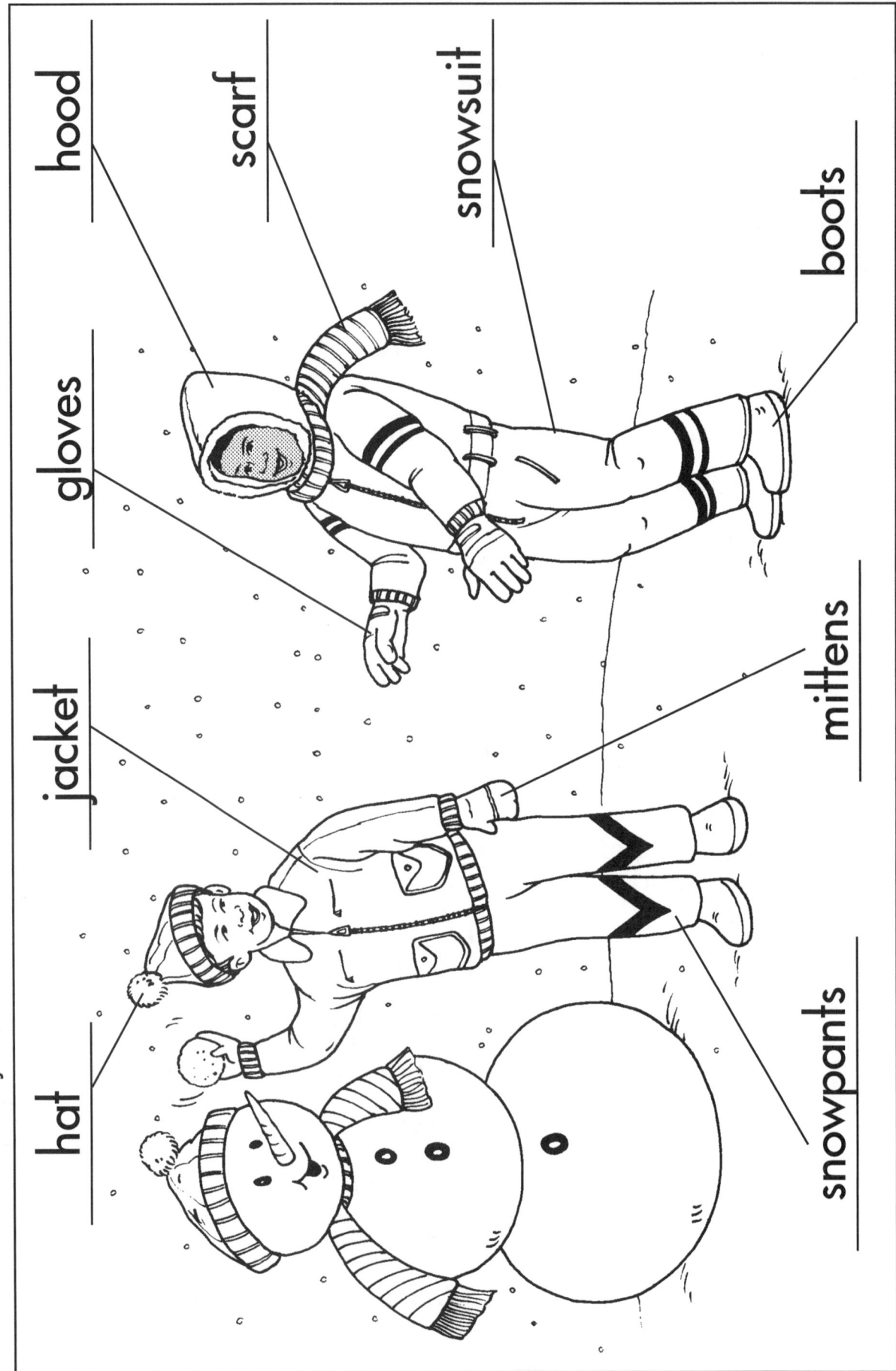

It's Cold 1, cont.

Write the word for each object pictured.

It's Cold 2

Here are some words for you to use.

snowpants	snowsuit	jacket
boots	scarf	hat
mittens	gloves	hood

Write the word for each object.

It's Cold 3

Name: _____

Complete each sentence.

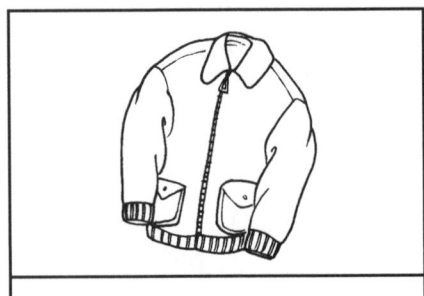 See the _____.

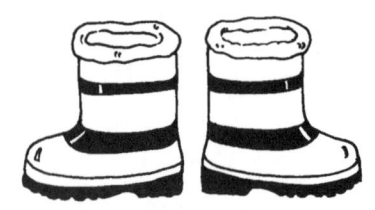 See the _____.

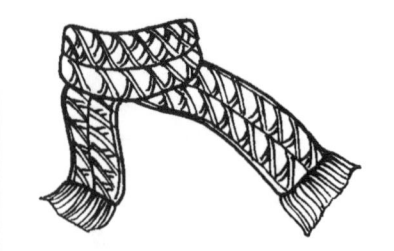 See the _____.

 See the _____.

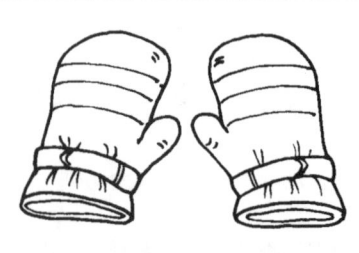 See the _____.

 See the _____.

It's Cold 4

Complete each sentence.

See the _____.
(T-shirt   skirt)

See the _____.
(raincoat   pants)

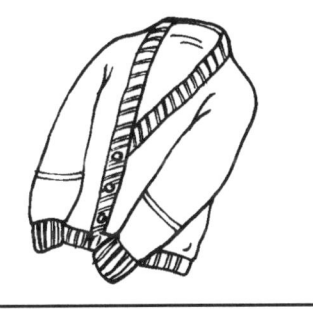

See the _____.
(skirt   sweater)

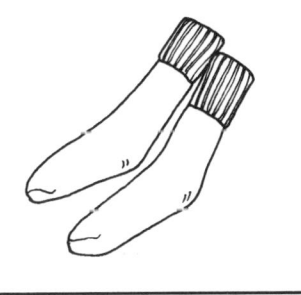

See the _____.
(socks   shoes)

See the _____.
(dress   shirt)

Write each word in the correct column.

A Hot Day

A Cold Day

_____

_____

_____

_____

_____

_____

_____

_____

_____

_____

swimsuit   scarf
jacket   T-shirt
mittens   sandals
gloves   sun hat
cap   snowsuit
shorts   snowpants

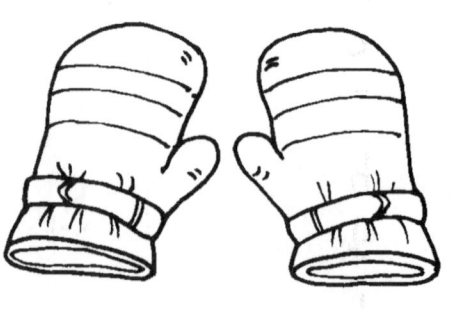

It's Cold 6

Circle each correct answer.

1. Which one of these is worn around your neck?
   a. scarf   b. snowsuit   c. boots
   d. gloves   e. hat

2. Which one of these would you wear if it was cold outside?
   a. swimsuit   b. sandals   c. sun hat
   d. shorts   e. snowsuit

3. Which one of these has fingers?
   a. hood   b. jacket   c. gloves
   d. scarf   e. mittens

4. Which one of these has a thumb?
   a. socks   b. mittens   c. cap
   d. scarf   e. hood

5. Which one of these will keep your feet warm?
   a. sandals   b. snowpants   c. hat
   d. boots   e. mittens

6. Which one of these might have a hood?
   a. jacket   b. scarf   c. socks
   d. hat   e. pants

Name:

Fill in the blank.

1. The children put the long _____ around the snowman's neck.

2. Put on your _____ to keep your legs warm.

3. His _____ covers his whole body and keeps him warm.

4. _____ keep your feet warm when you walk in the snow.

5. Her _____ have holes in the fingers.

6. Gloves or _____ will keep your hands warm.

7. That short _____ has a hood.

8. Put up your _____ to keep your head warm.

9. The boys put a black _____ on the snowman's head.

gloves
mittens
hat
scarf
snowsuit
snowpants
hood
jacket
boots

Name:

Read the word for each object pictured.

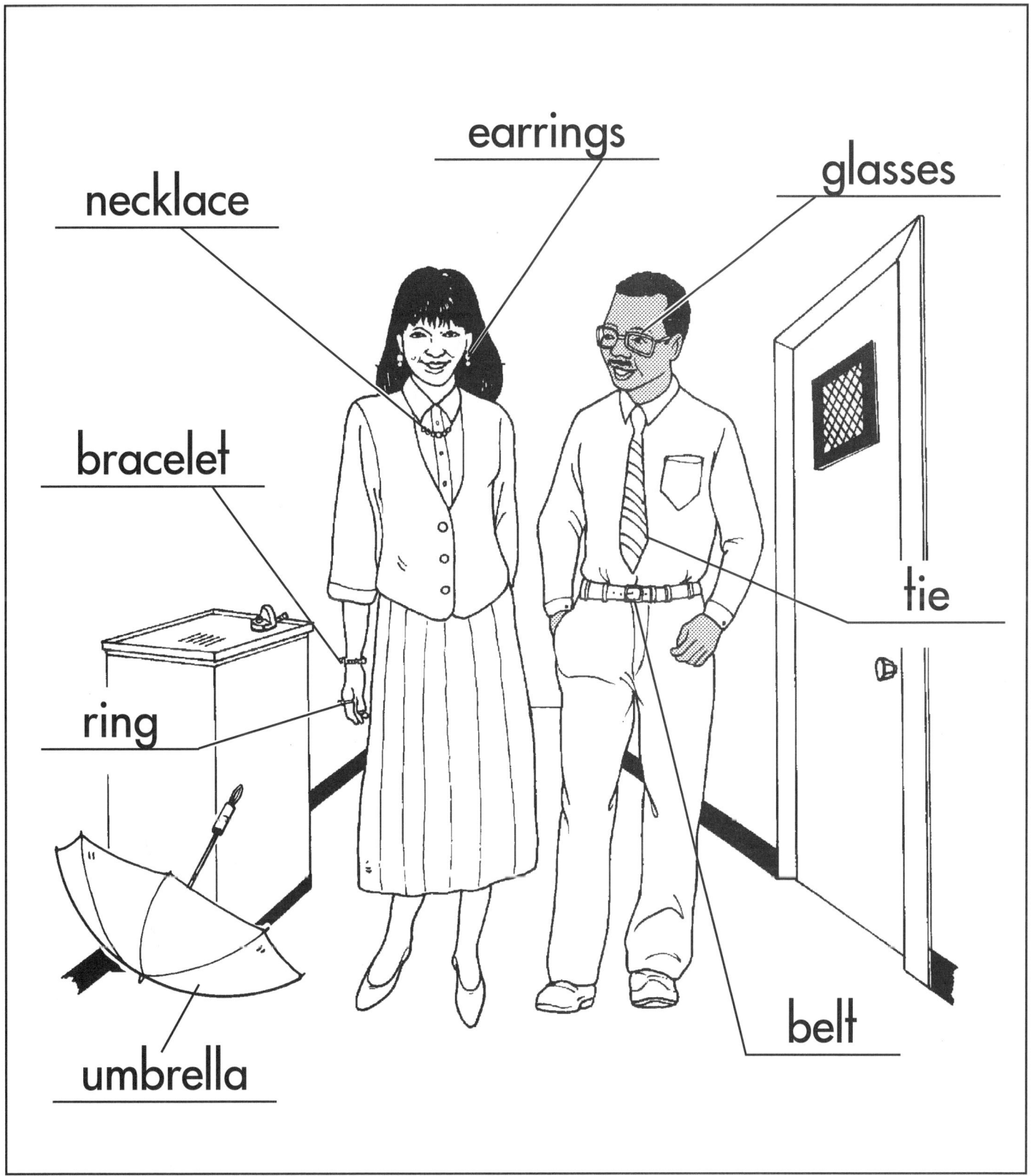

earrings

glasses

necklace

bracelet

ring

umbrella

tie

belt

Accessories 1, cont.

Name:

Write the word for each object pictured.

Accessories 2

Here are some words for you to use.

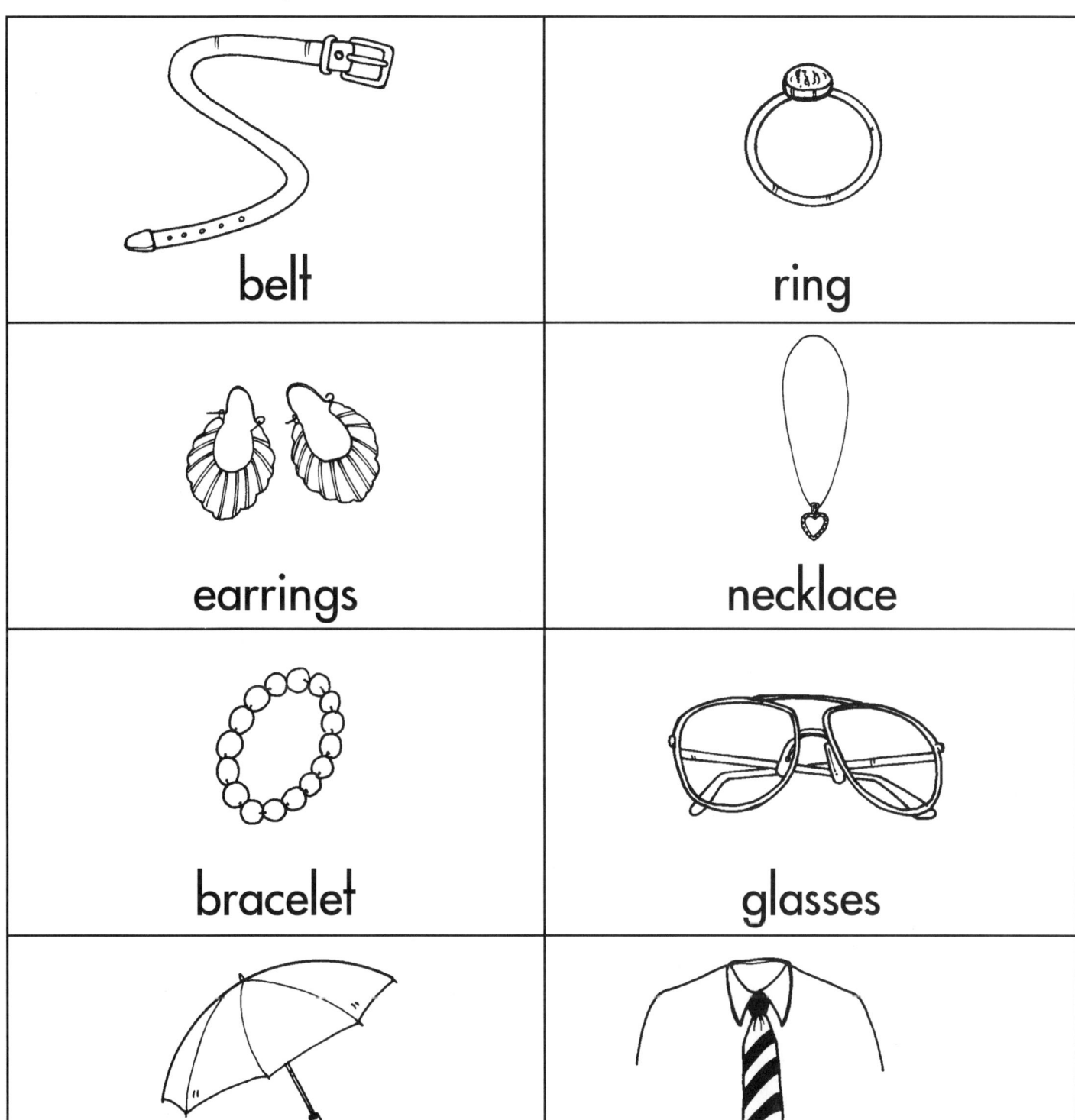

belt	ring
earrings	necklace
bracelet	glasses
umbrella	tie

115

Name: _____

Write the word for each object.

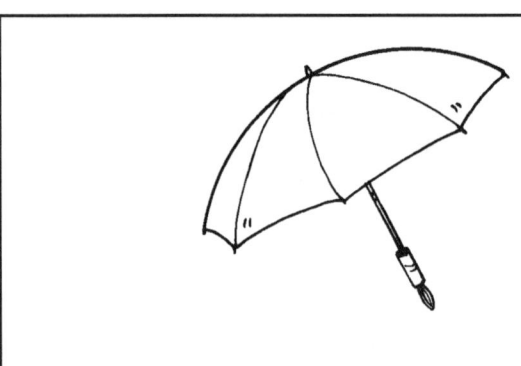

_____

_____

_____

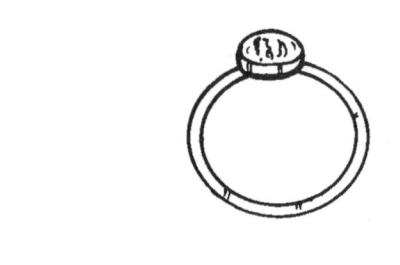

_____

_____

_____

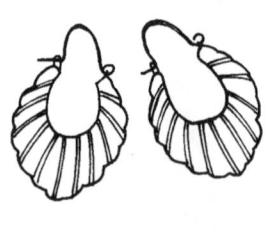

_____

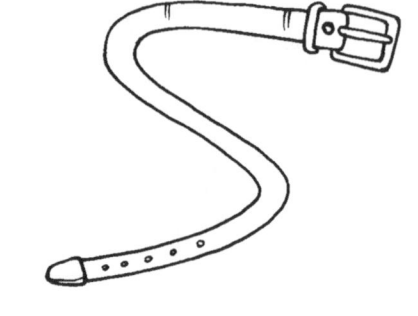

_____

Accessories 3

Complete each sentence.

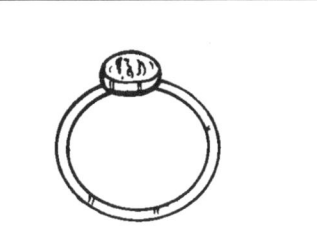

She likes her _____.

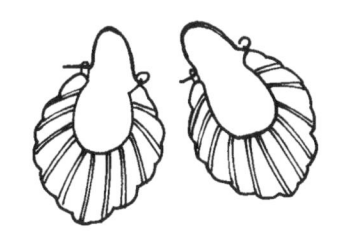

She likes her _____.

She likes her _____.

He likes his _____.

He likes his _____.

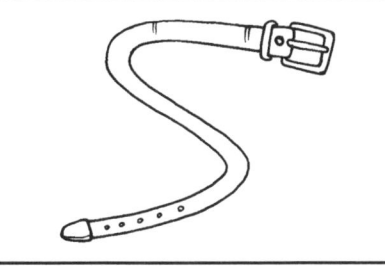

He likes his _____.

Accessories 4

Name: _____

Write **yes** or **no** for each statement.

yes   no

1. Here is a belt.  _____

2. Here is a ring. 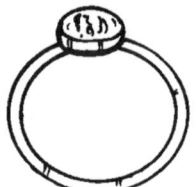 _____

3. Here are earrings. 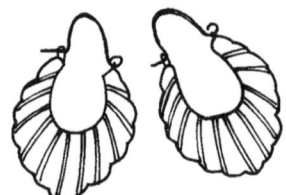 _____

4. Here is a necklace.  _____

5. Here is an umbrella.  _____

Name:

Write **yes** or **no** for each statement.

yes   **no**

1. Here are glasses.      _____

2. Here is an umbrella.   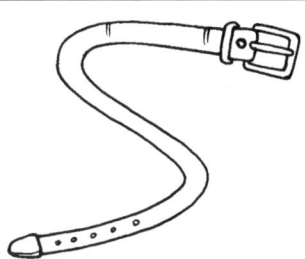   _____

3. Here is a tie.      _____

4. Here is a ring.      _____

5. Here is a bracelet.      _____

Accessories 5

Circle the correct answer.

1. Which one of these keeps us dry?
   a. necklace   b. belt   c. bracelet
   d. tie   e. umbrella

2. Which one of these could be made of gold?
   a. ring   b. tie   c. umbrella
   d. jacket   e. boots

3. Which one of these helps us see?
   a. ring   b. necklace   c. sweater
   d. glasses   e. hat

4. Which one of these could you wear with a shirt?
   a. blouse   b. dress   c. tie
   d. umbrella   e. shirt

5. Which one of these goes around your wrist?
   a. glasses   b. bracelet   c. tie
   d. ring   e. earring

6. Which one of these do you wear to hold up your pants?
   a. boots   b. belt   c. mittens
   d. necklace   e. bracelet

Accessories 6

Fill in the blank.

1. Her _____ fell off her wrist.

2. He only wears his _____ when he reads.

3. Take your _____ because it is raining.

4. The _____ around his waist holds up his pants.

5. Look at the gold _____ on his finger.

6. Mom wears a red _____ around her neck.

7. Is she wearing _____ in her ears?

8. He bought a shirt and _____ to go with his new suit.

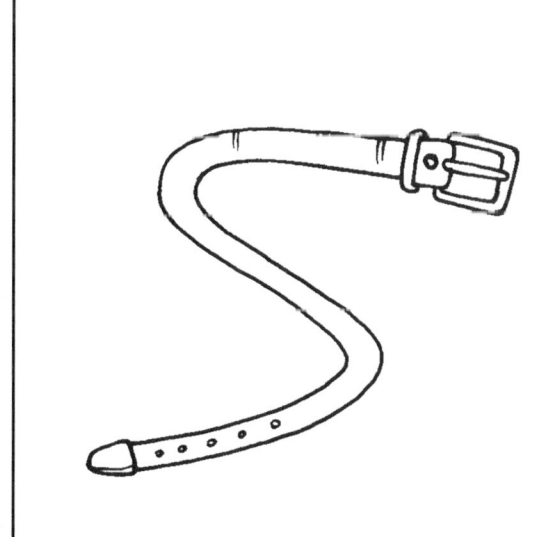

earrings
bracelet
glasses
tie
necklace
belt
ring
umbrella

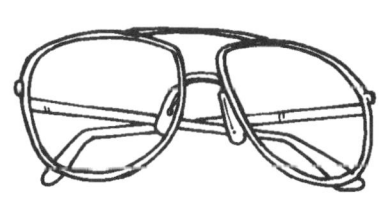

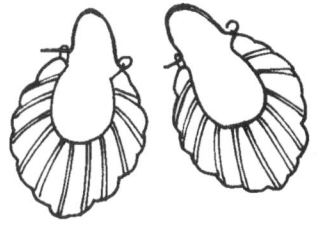

Bits and Pieces 1

Read the word for each object pictured.

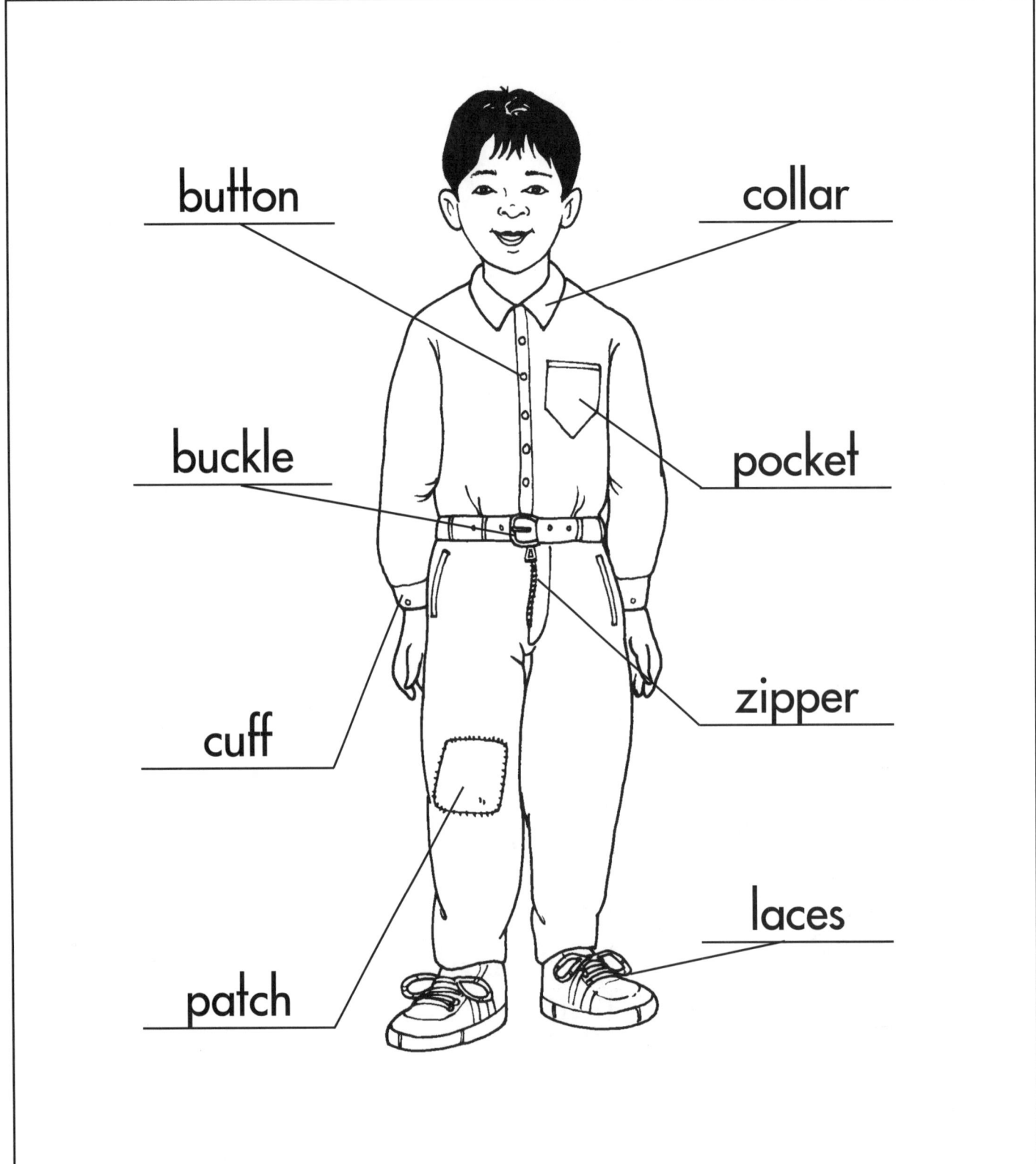

button

collar

buckle

pocket

cuff

zipper

patch

laces

Write the word for each object pictured.

Bits and Pieces 2

Here are some words for you to use.

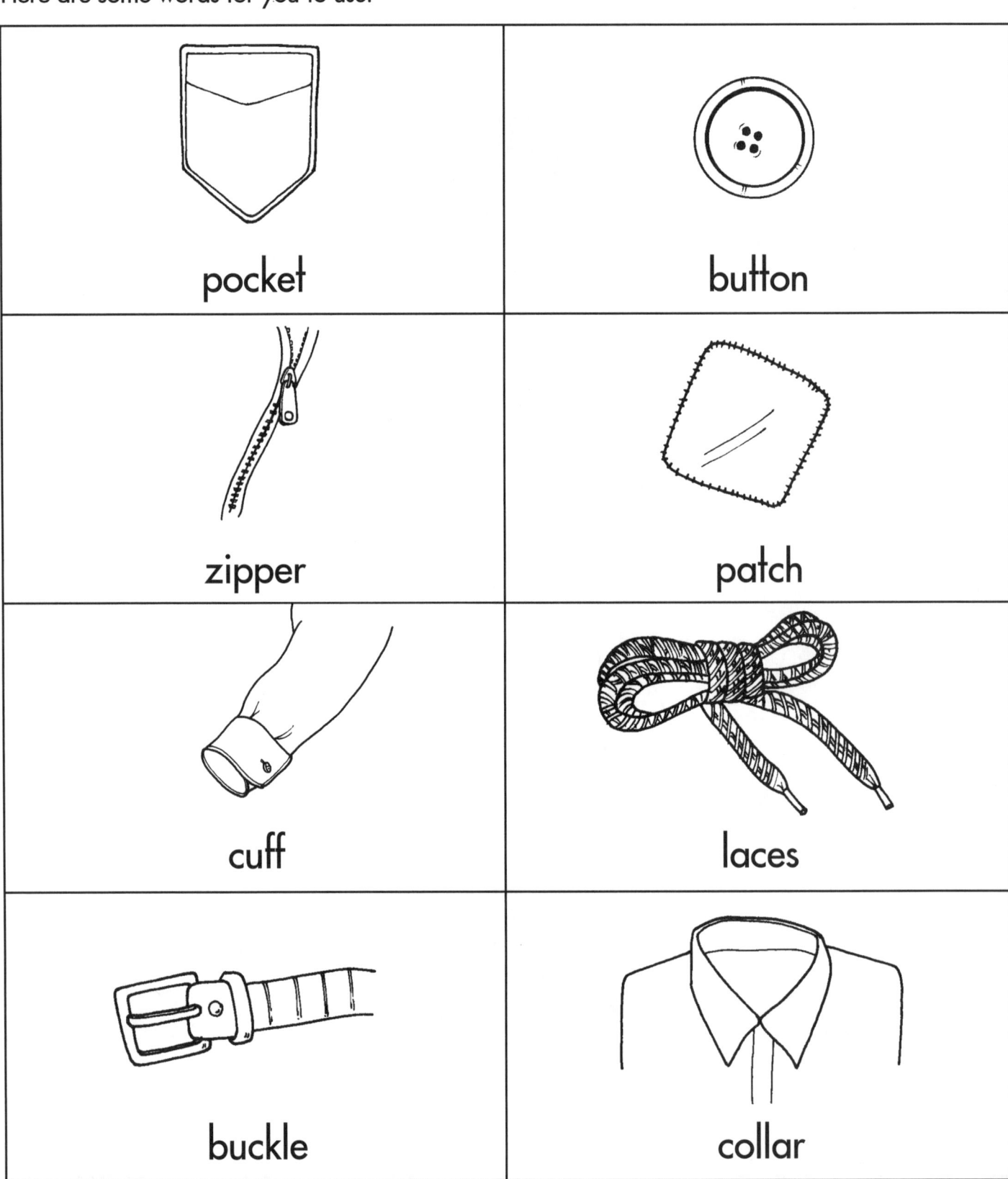

pocket	button
zipper	patch
cuff	laces
buckle	collar

Bits and Pieces 2, cont.

Write the word for each object.

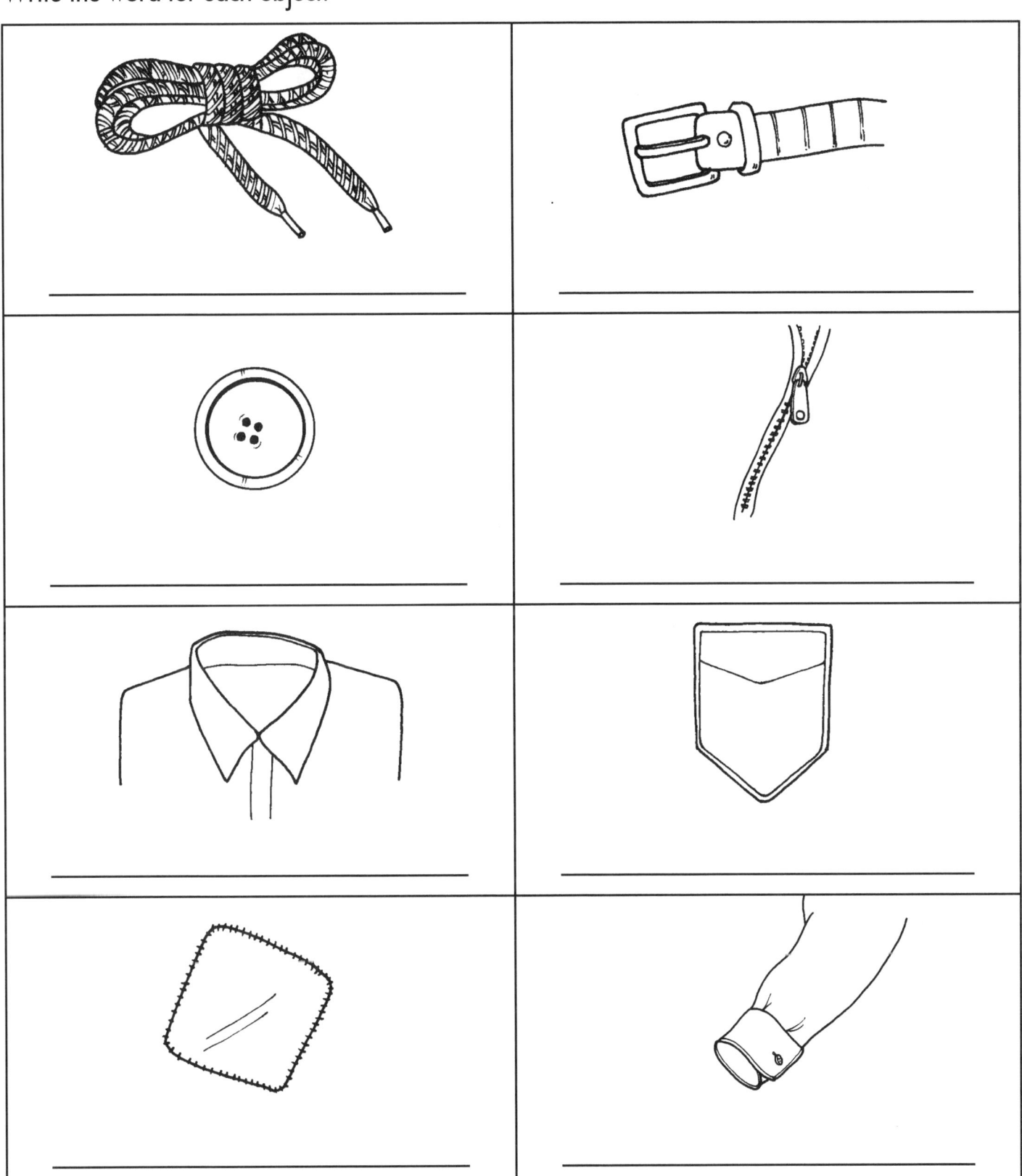

Bits and Pieces 3

Complete each sentence.

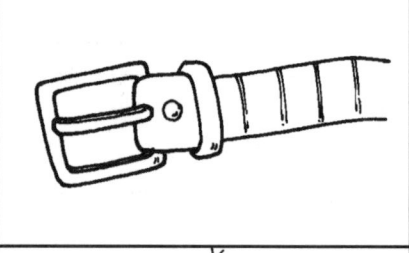

I can see a_____.

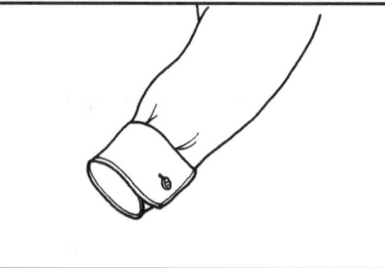

I can see a_____.

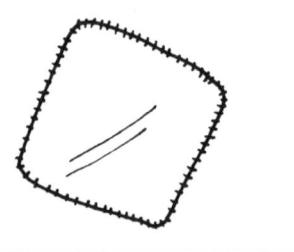

I can see a_____.

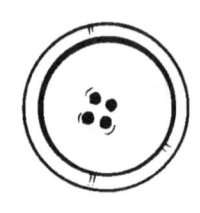

I can see a_____.

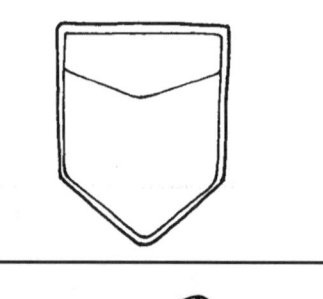

I can see a_____.

I can see _____.

Bits and Pieces 4

Complete each sentence.

1. I like her _____.
   (ring   glasses)

2. I like her _____.
   (bracelet   belt)

3. I like his _____.
   (necklace   glasses)

4. I like her _____.
   (tie   earrings)

5. I like his _____.
   (pocket   ring)

6. I like his _____.
   (umbrella   collar)

7. I like her _____.
   (umbrella   pocket)

8. I like his _____.
   (bracelet   tie)

9. I like her _____.
   (necklace   buckle)

10. I like his _____.
    (belt   ring)

11. I like his _____.
    (necklace   buckle)

Bits and Pieces 5

Write **yes** or **no** for each statement.

The belt is **around** her waist.

	yes	no

1. A belt goes around the waist. _____
2. An umbrella goes around the leg. _____
3. A ring goes around the finger. _____
4. Laces go around the arm. _____
5. A pocket goes around a dress. _____
6. A necklace goes around the neck. _____
7. A collar goes around the neck. _____
8. A bracelet goes around the hips. _____
9. A button goes around a shirt. _____
10. A tie goes around the neck. _____

Bits and Pieces 6

Circle each correct answer.

1. Which one of these do we use to tie our shoes?
    a. collar   b. pocket   c. laces
    d. patch   e. cuff

2. Which one of these do you find at the bottom of a pant leg?
    a. cuff   b. buckle   c. pocket
    d. gloves   e. umbrella

3. Which one of these do you sew over a hole in clothing?
    a. earrings   b. buckle   c. collar
    d. patch   e. laces

4. Which one of these is part of a belt?
    a. buckle   b. cuff   c. laces
    d. collar   e. button

5. Which one of these is used to carry things?
    a. patch   b. button   c. pocket
    d. laces   e. necklace

6. Which one of these is usually round?
    a. shoes   b. zipper   c. gloves
    d. sandals   e. button

Bits and Pieces 7

Name: _____

Fill in the blank.

1. Dad sewed a _____ on the knee of my pants.

2. Zip up the _____ on your jacket.

3. The _____ on his belt is silver.

4. I had to sew a round _____ on my shirt.

5. Do you carry your car keys in your _____ ?

6. The fold of cloth at the bottom of a pair of pants is

   called a _____ .

7. Tie the _____ on your shoes or you might fall down.

8. Her new dress has a purple _____ around
   the neck.

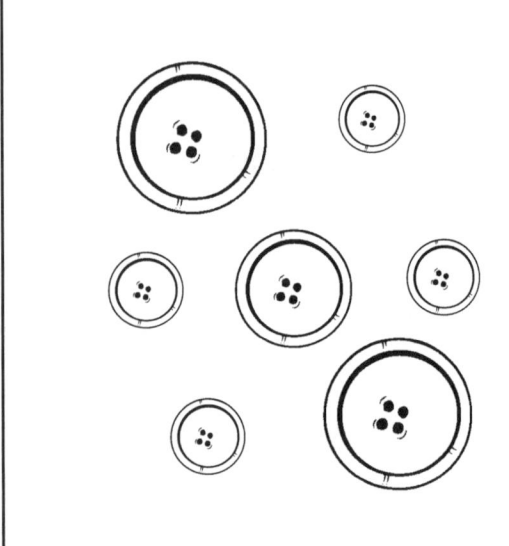

pocket
button
collar
zipper
patch
buckle
laces
cuff

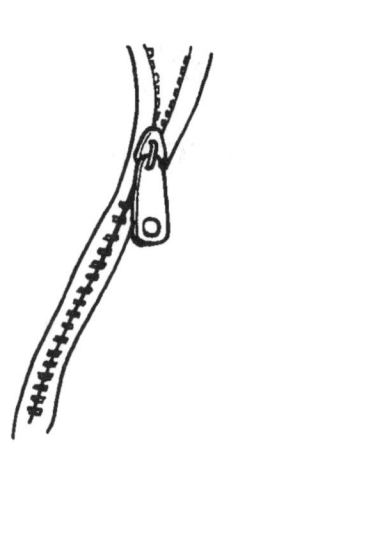

Vocabulary List

Part 2

barefoot	nightgown	slippers
barrette	overalls	sneakers
bathrobe	pajamas	suit
bow	pantyhose	suspenders
coat	parka	sweatshirt
diaper	ribbon	thongs
flippers	rubber boots	tights
headband	seam	undershirt
hem	skates	underwear
jeans	skis	velcro
jogging suit	sleeve	vest
moccasins	slip	windbreaker

Following Directions 1

Name:

Read each direction and see how it's used.

draw	buckle	
color		
write	raincoat	<u>raincoat</u>
fill in the blanks	The <u>skirt</u> is <u>blue</u> .	
cross out	earrings necklace ~~pants~~ ring	
underline	earrings necklace <u>pants</u> ring	
circle	earrings necklace (pants) ring	
copy	shorts <u>shorts</u>	
match	snow pants glasses sun hat snowpants glasses sun hat	
label	<u>pants</u> <u>patch</u> <u>pocket</u>	

Follow each direction.

color	
cross out	blouse bracelet shirt T-shirt
circle	skirt dress blouse umbrella
draw	T-shirt
fill in the blank	boots necklace I put a pair of _____ on my feet.
copy	snowsuit _____

Follow each direction.

write	earrings _____
underline	hood socks shoes boots
fill in the blank	jacket zipper The _____ has a hood.
match	sweater gloves glasses glasses gloves sweater
cross out	hat tie cap hood
label	_____ _____ _____

Name:

Follow each direction.

draw:	necklace, bracelet, cap, T-shirt
write:	your name on the store's sign
cross out:	snowsuit
circle:	bracelet
underline:	swimsuit
label:	necklace
color:	the picture

Personal Clothes 1

Name:

Here are some words for you to use.

pajamas

bathrobe

underwear

undershirt

nightgown

slip

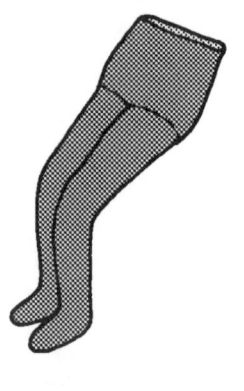

tights

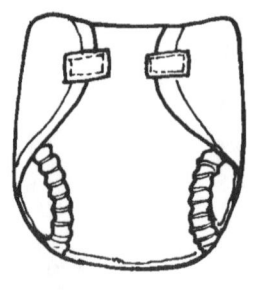

diaper

pantyhose

Personal Clothes 2

Follow the directions.

underline: underwear, pajamas

cross out: undershirt, bathrobe

circle: pantyhose, diaper

pajamas	bathrobe	underwear	undershirt	nightgown
slip	tights	diaper	pantyhose	slip	diaper	tights
slip	nightgown	undershirt	underwear	bathrobe
pajamas	tights	undershirt	pajamas	diaper	nightgown
bathrobe	underwear	pantyhose	pajamas	bathrobe
underwear	undershirt	nightgown	slip	tights	diaper
pantyhose	underwear	bathrobe	pajamas	slip	nightgown
undershirt	pantyhose	diaper	tights	underwear	slip
pantyhose	bathrobe	nightgown	diaper	pajamas
undershirt	tights	pantyhose	slip	underwear	bathrobe
nightgown	diaper	pajamas	undershirt	tights	slip
pantyhose	diaper	tights	slip	nightgown	pajamas

Personal Clothes 3

Name:

Mark **true** or **false** for each statement.

1. Birds wear diapers. __true __false

2. An undershirt might keep you warm. __true __false

3. A woman might wear a slip under her dress. __true __false

4. Pajamas are usually worn at bedtime. __true __false

5. Pantyhose are worn on the legs. __true __false

6. You wear a bathrobe on the bus. __true __false

7. Tights might keep a person's legs warm. __true __false

8. You might wear a nightgown to play hockey. __true __false

9. You wear underwear over your pants. __true __false

Personal Clothes 4

Complete each sentence. Then, write the sentence.

He, his   She, her

1. ____ is wearing _____ pajamas.

_____

2. ____ is wearing _____ pajamas.

_____

3. ____ is wearing _____ slip.

_____

4. ____ is wearing _____ bathrobe.

_____

5. ____ is wearing _____ undershirt.

_____

Personal Clothes 5

Fill in the blank.

1. Who is going to change the baby's _____?

2. Her big sister wore _____ with her high heels.

3. _____ are good things to wear in bed.

4. After my shower, I put on a _____.

5. You wear _____ under your pants.

6. She needed a long _____ to wear under her long dress.

7. You can wear an _____ under your shirt.

8. The little girl wore red _____ to keep her legs warm.

9. Did she wear her _____ or pajamas to bed?

pantyhose	diaper	tights
slip	nightgown	undershirt
pajamas	underwear	bathrobe

Outside Clothes 1

Here are some words for you to use.

coat

windbreaker

parka

suit

jeans

jogging suit

sweatshirt

vest

overalls

Outside Clothes 2

Name: _____

Write each word twice.

coat   _____   _____

windbreaker   _____   _____

parka   _____   _____

suit   _____   _____

jeans   _____   _____

jogging suit   _____   _____

sweatshirt   _____   _____

vest   _____   _____

overalls   _____   _____

Outside Clothes 3

Name:

Underline the correct spelling of each word. Then, write the word three times.

Underline		Write
windbreaker	windbraker	_____
windbreaker	windbreeker	_____
windbreaker	wyndbreaker	_____
windbreakir	windbreaker	_____
jogging suit	jogging suit	_____
jogging soot	joging suit	_____
jogging suit	joggeng suit	_____
jogging suite	jogging siut	_____
sweetshirt	sweatshurt	_____
sweatshirt	swetshirt	_____
sweatshirt	swaetshirt	_____
sweatshirt	sweatshirt	_____
overals	oviralls	_____
overalls	ovuralls	_____
overalls	overalls	_____
overills	overalls	_____

Outside Clothes 4

Name: _____

Mark **true** or **false** for each statement.

1. A windbreaker blows leaves off trees.   __true   __false

2. A vest has two legs.   __true   __false

3. People wear parkas at the beach on a hot day.   __true   __false

4. Overalls usually have straps to hold them up.   __true   __false

5. You might put on a coat to go outside.   __true   __false

6. Blue jeans can be worn to a football game.   __true   __false

7. A sweatshirt makes you feel colder.   __true   __false

8. A suit can come in two or three pieces.   __true   __false

9. Some people wear a jogging suit when they run.   __true   __false

Outside Clothes 5

Name:

Draw a picture for eight of your new words. Then, write the word.

coat   windbreaker   parka
suit   jeans   jogging suit
sweatshirt   vest   overalls

_____   _____

_____   _____

_____   _____

_____   _____

Outside Clothes 6

Name: _____

Write a sentence for each picture.

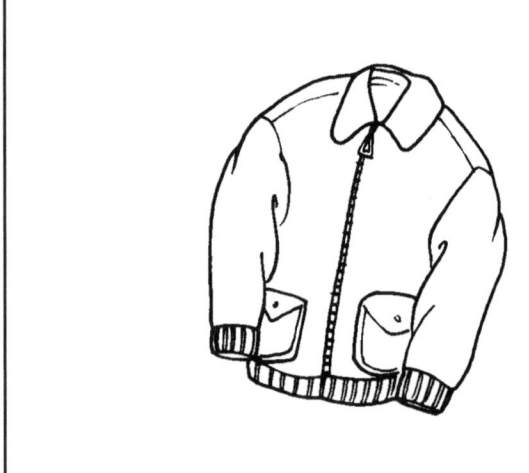

_____

_____

_____

_____

_____

_____

_____

_____

Outside Clothes 7

Name: _____

Fill in the blank.

1. I put on my hat and _____ before I go out in the cold weather.

2. Dad's _____ has a jacket, pants, and a vest.

3. Mom likes the _____ that goes with her new green jogging suit.

4. My sister wears her jean jacket with blue _____.

5. When it is very cold, I pull up the hood of my _____.

6. He wants to go running in his red _____ but he can't find the pants.

7. I wear my _____ on a windy day.

8. She wears her sleeveless _____ with her best skirt and blouse.

9. Fasten the straps on your _____.

overalls	vest	sweatshirt
jogging suit	jeans	suit
windbreaker	parka	coat

On Your Feet 1

Name:

Here are some words for you to use.

slippers

sneakers

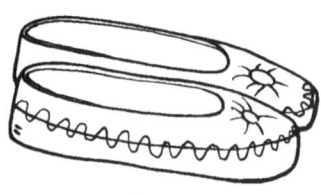

moccasins

rubber boots

thongs

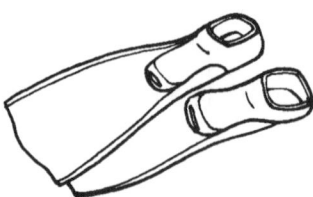

flippers

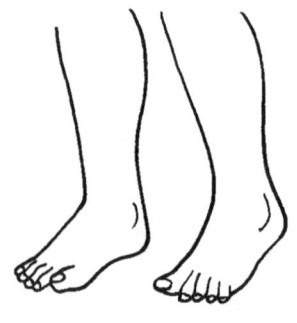

barefoot

skates

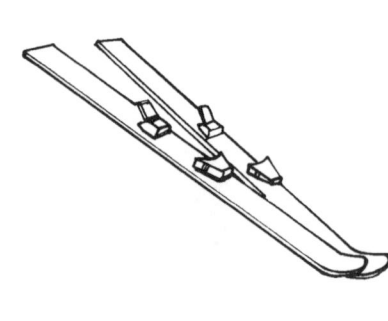

skis

Write each word twice.

slippers   _____   _____

sneakers   _____   _____

moccasins   _____   _____

rubber boots _____   _____

thongs   _____   _____

flippers   _____   _____

barefoot   _____   _____

skates   _____   _____

skis   _____   _____

On Your Feet 3

Name: _____

Mark **true** or **false** for each statement.

1. Slippers can be worn at home.   __true   __false

2. When you are barefoot, you are wearing shoes.   __true   __false

3. Flippers are usually made of rubber.   __true   __false

4. Skis help you go down a snowy hill.   __true   __false

5. Moccasins will help you move faster in the water.   __true   __false

6. Skates have blades.   __true   __false

7. You might eat thongs for breakfast.   __true   __false

8. Sneakers can help you run faster.   __true   __false

9. Rubber boots usually come in pairs.   __true   __false

 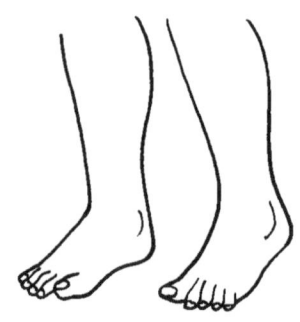

On Your Feet 4

Fill in each blank.

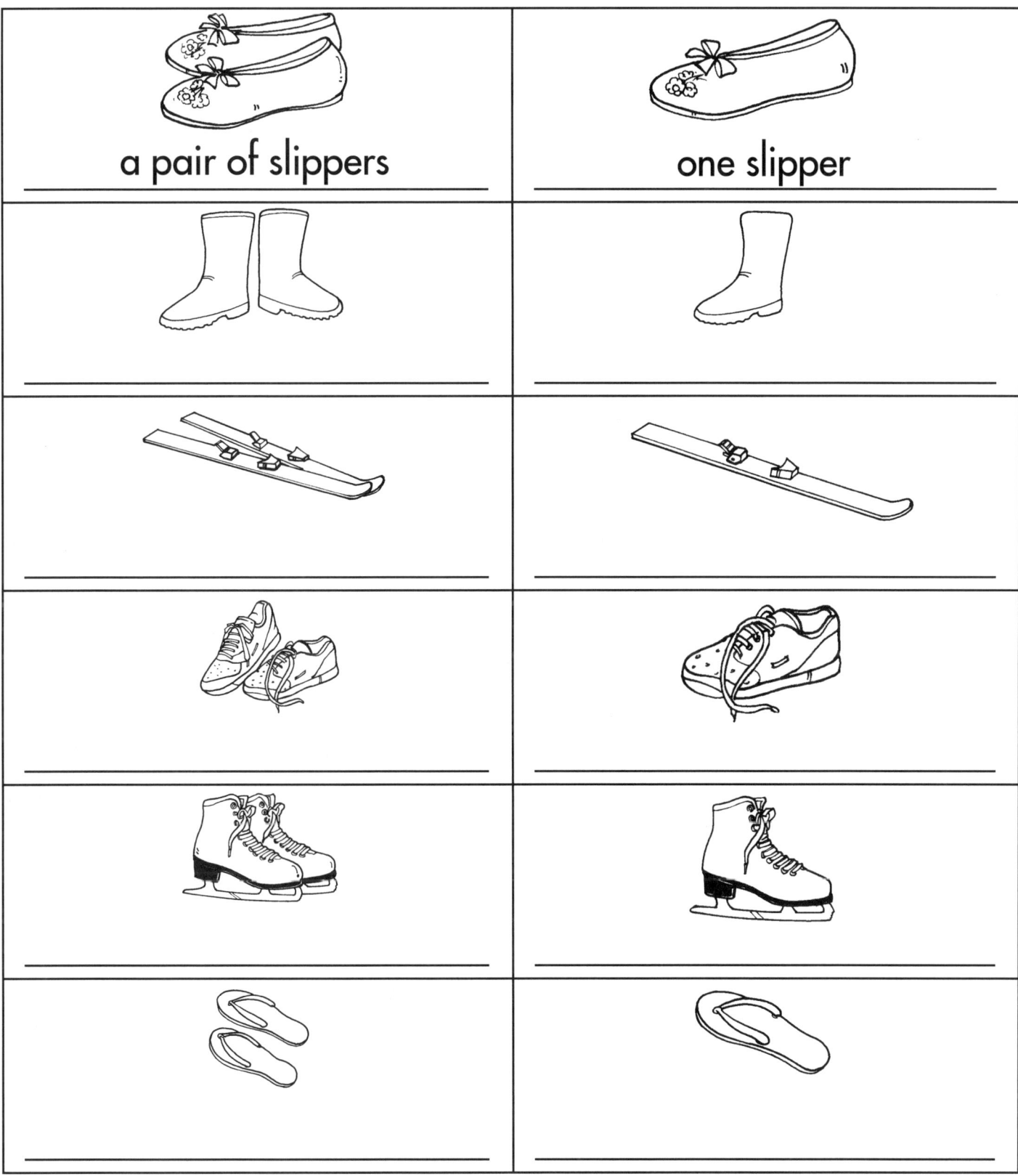

a pair of slippers

one slipper

Name:

Complete each sentence.

On my feet, I like to wear a pair of ____

_____

On my feet, I like to wear a pair _____

_____

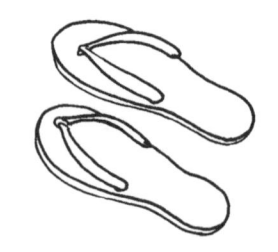

On my feet, I like to wear _____

_____

On my feet, I like _____

_____

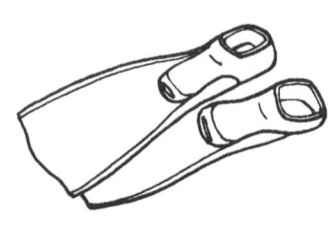

On my feet, _____

_____

On _____

_____

On Your Feet 6

Fill in the blank.

1. In the winter, I take my _____ and ski poles to the hill.

2. The patterns on the soft leather _____ were made with beads.

3. I like to feel the sand between my toes when I walk _____ on the beach.

4. My brother wears _____ to help him swim.

5. My sister's _____ make a funny sound as she walks along the beach.

6. We walk through the puddles in our raincoats and _____ _____.

7. After my bath, I put on my _____ and bathrobe.

8. Do you wear your _____ and jogging suit when you run?

9. Sharpen your _____ before you play hockey.

slippers	sneakers	moccasins
rubber boots	thongs	flippers
barefoot	skates	skis

Name:

Here are some words for you to use.

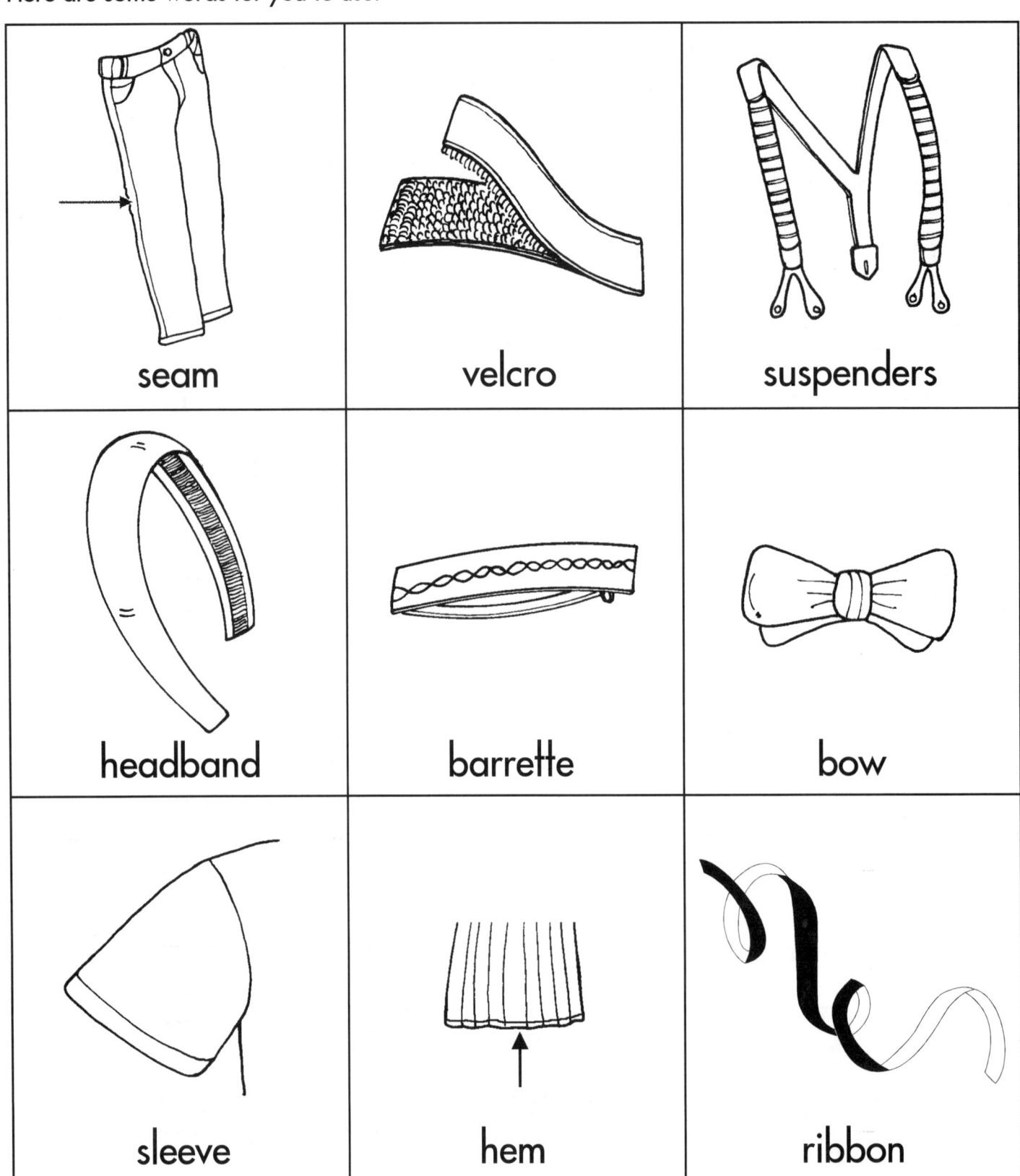

seam	velcro	suspenders
headband	barrette	bow
sleeve	hem	ribbon

More Bits and Pieces 2

Name: _____

Underline the correct spelling of each word. Then, write the word three times.

Underline	Write
barrette barette	_____
barrette barrete	_____
barrett barrette	_____
barrette barete	_____
suspinders suspenders	_____
suspernders suspenders	_____
saspenders suspendirs	_____
suspenders suspenders	_____
headband hedband	_____
haedband headbend	_____
headband headband	_____
headband heaband	_____
sleive sleave	_____
slieve sleeve	_____
sleeve sleeve	_____
sleefe sleeve	_____

More Bits and Pieces 3

Name: _____

Mark **true** or **false** for each statement.

1. Suspenders usually go over the shoulders.   __true   __false

2. A barrette can hold hair in place.   __true   __false

3. Ribbon comes in many colors.   __true   __false

4. A hem is a fold at the bottom of a dress.   __true   __false

5. Velcro helps us to see better.   __true   __false

6. It's easy to tie a bow with one hand.   __true   __false

7. A headband is worn on your heels.   __true   __false

8. A seam joins two pieces of cloth together.   __true   __false

9. A sleeve is usually seen on a vest.   __true   __false

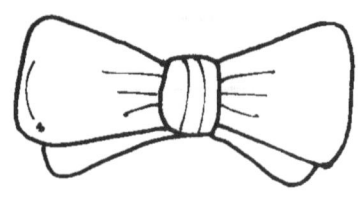 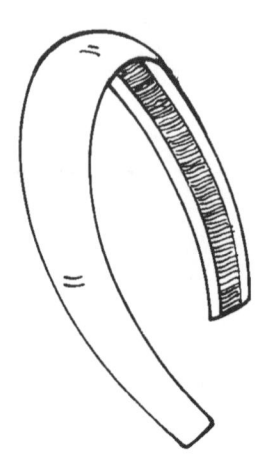 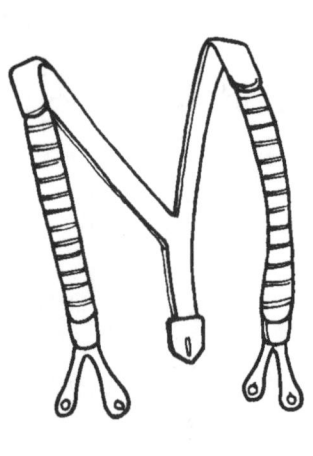

More Bits and Pieces 4

Name:

Cross out the eight mistakes in this story. Write the correct word above each mistake.

My sister was going shopping. She didn't buy one dress because the pants were too long for her arms. The hood on the bottom of the dress was not straight, and she didn't like the color of the necklace around the waist.

Next, she looked at a pair of pants with shoes to hold them up. The scarf on the leg was coming apart. She liked one pair of shoes, but they had collars instead of laces. She looked at a ribbon for her hair, but they were all too small.

At last, she found something she liked. She bought a green and blue swimsuit for her head. Shopping is a lot of work!

seam	velcro	suspenders
headband	barrette	bow
sleeves	hem	ribbon

More Bits and Pieces 5

Name: _____

Write a sentence using each of these words.

1. seam _____

_____

2. suspenders _____

_____

3. headband _____

_____

4. barrette _____

_____

5. bow _____

_____

6. sleeve _____

_____

7. hem _____

_____

8. ribbon _____

_____

More Bits and Pieces 6

Fill in the blank.

1. Her dress has a pretty pink _____ made of ribbon.

2. Mom sewed the _____ at the bottom of her new skirt.

3. Dad had to sew the _____ on his pants because it came apart.

4. One _____ of his shirt had a hole in it.

5. The tiny, plastic _____ keeps her hair away from her face.

6. My sister put a new red _____ around her sun hat.

7. My mom puts a _____ around her head to keep her hair back.

8. I fasten my shoes with _____ instead of laces.

9. He holds his pants up with red _____.

seam	velcro	suspenders
headband	barrette	bow
sleeve	hem	ribbon

Extension Activity 1

Name:

Make a list for each category.

Material used to make clothes

_____   _____

_____   _____

_____   _____

_____   _____

Special clothes for sports

_____   _____

_____   _____

_____   _____

People who wear uniforms

_____   _____

_____   _____

_____   _____

Extension Activity 2

Make a list for each category.

Clothes worn in the summer

_____   _____

_____   _____

_____   _____

_____   _____

Clothes worn in other countries

_____   _____

_____   _____

_____   _____

_____   _____

Clothes worn by babies

_____   _____

_____   _____

_____   _____

_____   _____

Name:

What would you wear to:

a wedding _____

school _____

a swimming pool _____

the mall _____

visit relatives _____

the gym _____

play your favorite sport _____

Vocabulary Picture Cards

dress	skirt	blouse
shirt	pants	shoes
sweater	raincoat	shorts
T-shirt	swimsuit	sandals

Vocabulary Picture Cards, cont.

sun hat	socks	cap
snowsuit	snowpants	jacket
boots	scarf	hat
mittens	gloves	hood

Vocabulary Picture Cards, cont.

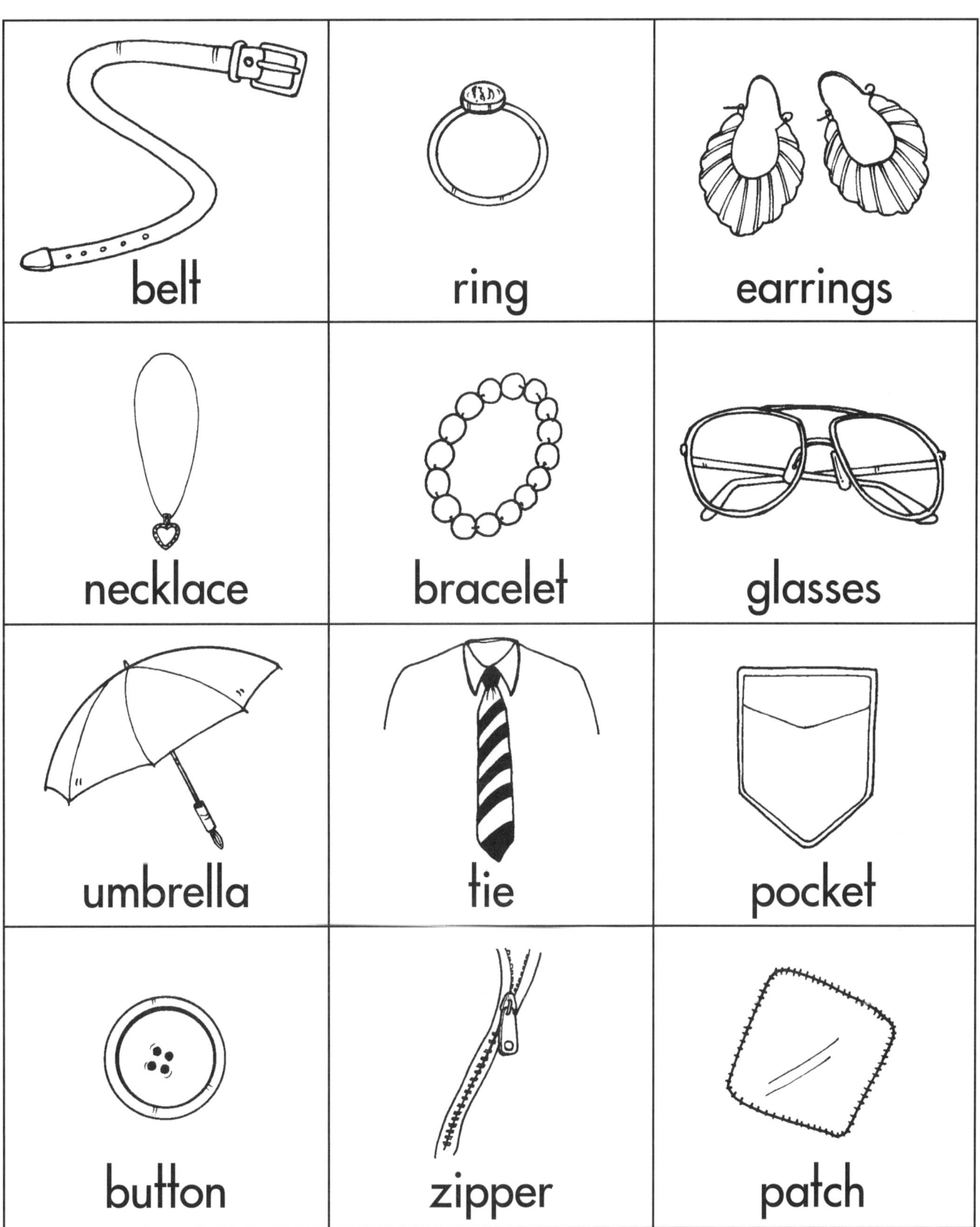

belt	ring	earrings
necklace	bracelet	glasses
umbrella	tie	pocket
button	zipper	patch

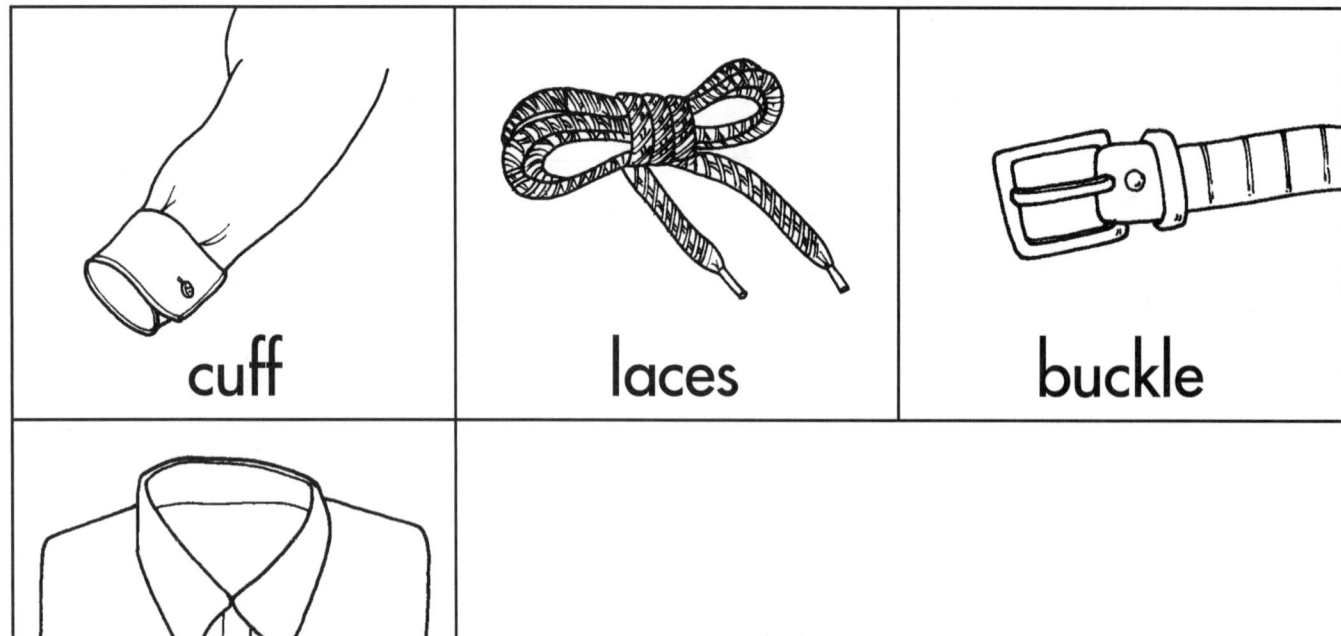

cuff

laces

buckle

collar

19-03-987654321